THE MAN IN THE CRACKED MIRROR!

LAMONT BERSHAWN

Copyright © 2020 by Lamont Bershawn.

ISBN   978-1-970160-66-6   Ebook
ISBN   978-1-970160-67-3   Paperback

All rights reserved. No part of this publication may be reproduced, distributed, or transmitted in any form or by any means, including photocopying, recording, or other electronic or mechanical methods without the prior written permission of the publisher. For permission requests, solicit the publisher via the address below through mail or email with the subject line "Attention: Publication Permission".

The EC Publishing LLC books may be ordered
through booksellers or by contacting:

EC Publishing LLC
116 South Magnolia Ave.
Suite 3, Unit F
Ocala, FL 34471, USA
Direct Line: +1 (352) 644-6538
Fax: +1 (800) 483-1813
http://www.ecpublishingllc.com/

Ordering Information:
Quantity sales. Special discounts are available on quantity purchases by corporations, associations, and others. For details, contact the publisher at the address above.

Printed in the United States of America

CONTENTS

You Are A King 1
Introduction 5
You'll Never Be Me 11
The Infancy Gospel 14
The Liar That Lingers in the Closet 26
Misery Poem 69
Misery 71
The Enemy Poem 100
The Enemy Tried to Devour My Inner-Me 101
Mama's Boy 152
My Mother Never Failed Me Poem 159
"I'm Still Your Brother" 161
"Acknowledgements" 163
"I'm Here for You Brother" 166

You Are A King

You are a king,
Whatever you do analyze everything,
The melanin in your skin,
Is a small reminder that you always win.

No matter what you set out to do,
They'll never expect it coming from you,
So, remember to keep things tight,
And never give up without a fight.
Be watchful of the slander coming from your friend or that which is considered your kin,
They have yet to understand the power of their melanin.
Continue to be bold and live a great life,
When they can't break you, they'll go through your wife.

Lamont Bershawn

Birthed from the royal priesthood,
Representing those young kings living in the hood.
Seeing a strong black man seems to be a tale,
When young black boys resort to visiting their fathers in the jail cell.

Racial injustices will always exist,
Your body is a target and they rarely do miss.
Brother, what in this world have you done?
Making it in this realm folk know that you've already won.

Please don't give up powerful kings,
The will of our ancestors are the wind blowing beneath your wings,
We were told that we could be anything from an astronaut to a nurse practitioner,
Chadwick you did your part, farewell Black Panther.

Marvel creates superheroes and comics,
A strange challenge that we must depict.
Leaving our children, a false sense of hope,
When the government systematically supplies the hood with dope.

The politician's campaign for that big paycheck,
Hiring racist cops that won't get up off the Negus neck. Making it easy to build a lifestyle selling drugs,
Getting thrown in the slammer being labeled thugs.

People of all races joined to be a force of one,
Speaking loudly to the injustice of black folk "We're Totally Done!"
All of a sudden here comes Covid-19,
If you look closely it's just another one of the government's schemes.

Little ones are being guided by religion,
Being molested by their faith which should have been a safe haven.
Destroying their dreams or kicking them out,
When they just wanted to learn how to be a Boy Scout.

You Are A King

This is why it's important for the world to see,
The melanin in my skin and the power within me.
Every ounce and fiber of my being,
Will prove to this prejudiced world that I am still a King!

- Lamont Bershawn (original piece)

INTRODUCTION

"The Man in the Cracked Mirror" is based on true events that have taken place over the years in my life being an identical twin. The cracked mirror symbolizes the broken relationship and brotherhood of a twin that's looked upon as your mirrored image, but is truly broken within.

Where did things go wrong?

How did the hate become so inevitable?

Will this bitterness ever end?

Will the lying ever stop?

These are some of the questions you'll ask while developing your own conclusion.

We all have the ability to control the negative as well as the positive things in our lives, with that being said it's hard to sit in the presence of negative energy and expect a positive outcome.

There's an old saying, "Keep your friends close but your enemies closer." It goes along with keeping a closer watch on those individuals that despise you and would do anything to cause your demise.

Don't ever be fooled into thinking or believing everyone is happy about your success, they're NOT.

As a matter of fact, there's those individuals that are hearing about your success or accomplishments that are ready and willing to put themselves in harm's way just as long as it becomes your demise.

Better yet, if a person will compromise your freedom or your life, they're not worth the air you breathe.

Sometimes forgiveness means to cut absolute ties with a person, group or organization!! - Lamont Bershawn.

You're going to see how easy it is to get manipulated and caught up in a web of lies and deceit. The moment that you feel the need to lie to an individual they're not receiving you, but the lie that you told them.

This is what I characterize or consider the actions of a "B.I.T.C.H." {Broke/Broken, Individual, Trying to Cause Havoc/Hell}. Throughout this true story you'll see me use a few acronyms that will define my perception in order to better describe an individual.

You'll also get a glimpse as to why a person seeks to destroy, discredit, degrade, devalue, disrespect and devour another's reputation and character.

And you always wished that you had a twin? I beg to differ!!

As you explore the pages keep in mind that you too have to make an account and take responsibility/ ownership of your actions. It is within my creative writing skills to enhance the boundaries of the closed mindset to accept the reality of life's circumstances.

As I engage in proactively expressing my distinct knowledge of the events that have taken place in my life, I'm disengaging the horror, conflict and ill will that it has caused me over the years.

You'll definitely understand why you wouldn't want to be wearing anyone else's shoes just by looking through the shattered glass into someone's proposed life!!

Let's take a closer look into the mirror. What do you see? If you're honest, you'll be able to see your very own reflection, blemishes, scars and imperfections.

When we take note and look at ourselves, our upbringing, how we were raised, the things we were taught, the people we considered a friend, those people we've considered a relative and our biological family member; we can see that there's a form of dysfunction present. Yes, we've either tried our best to cover up or protect someone and in the long run the shielding of them was nothing more than condoning their behavior.

Hiding, covering up, shielding or protecting an individual's sickness, faults or wrongdoing will only give the individual a green light to continue with their sadistic personality instead of seeking help.

Being born and growing up as an identical twin wasn't as fun for me as people would think. There are several types of twins: Fraternal, Conjoined, Identical, Polar Body {Half Identical}, Mixed Chromosome, Superfecundation and Superfetation.

The amazing thing about identical twins is that they're capable of playing tricks, playing each other roles, switching up and fooling people without people ever knowing the truth.

There have been several movies about the good, bad, evil and vindictive side of twins. One of the earlier and most famous movies about identical twins was called, "The Dark Mirror" starring Olivia de Havilland, 1946.

The horrifying idea that I could possibly be set up by my twin because we share the same DNA. If he has sex with a woman behind me and impregnate her, I could be blamed. Better yet, if I take a DNA test for his children I could pass as their father with a high percentage. Do you still wish that you were born as a twin?

This book is also being written for self-reflection and self-evaluation!!

"The Battle of the Gods!!"

And the voice of God came unto me unto me and said, "I WANT YOU TO GATHER ALL OF THE OTHER GODS SO WE CAN DETERMINE WHO'S ACTUALLY THE MOST POWERFUL OF THEM ALL."

I began sending emails, text messages, prayers, tarrying, smoke signals and chants just to see which "Gods" would show. To my surprise a few of them showed up. Being seated in my presence were:

(1) the Biblical God

(2) the "God" of ignorance

(3) Mammon

(4) Alcoholism

(5) Drug addiction

(6) Sexual addictions, etc.

The "Biblical" God responded with such force, "This is a no brainer. Don't you see that I've conquered a majority of the world? I have them mesmerized by my words."

"I beg to differ" said, Mammon. Don't you know I have people stealing, killing/ murdering and telling lies because of me?

Alcoholism responded, "I'm going to remove myself because I'm just a temporary fix that people tend to lean upon and get emotional."

Drug addiction put its two cents in to say, "Once a person takes a hit, I'll have them in the palm of my hands begging for me."

Sex addiction hollered out, "Hold up one damn second. I have people turning tricks, getting all types of diseases, destroying relationships/ marriages and the prime concern on these talk shows. Just look at Jerry Springer and Maury."

The "God" of ignorance laughed aloud and said, "I'm presented as truth and will continue to prey on the weak minded as long as they continue to allow the blind to lead them, allow the deaf to guide them and allow the dumb to speak to them."

As they were speaking among themselves, the room began to tremble with a thunderous sound as the "Voice" entered into the room laughing. The "Voice" responded to each of the other "gods."

"Biblical" God? How is it that you're the most powerful when your words couldn't put an end to slavery? BE GONE!!

"Mammon?" The greatest things on this planet have no use for you, they're PRICELESS!! BE GONE!!

"Alcoholism, Drug addiction, Sexual addiction?" {Before the "Voice" could respond they vanished}.

"Looks like it's between you {God of Ignorance} and me" said, the Voice.

The God of Ignorance stated, "You're powerful to those that knows how to tap into their own spirits to hear your VOICE, but I'm just as powerful to those that tap into their own spirits but REFUSE to take heed and therefore makes the decision to DENY truth. As the "Voice" began walking around the room full of mirrors it recognized, it was speaking with itself the entire time.

POINT: *The true battle is the battle that takes place within SELF!! - Lamont Bershawn.*

YOU'LL NEVER BE ME

Ever since we've been born you had something against me,
Was there something wrong with me you wanted the world to see?
Mom did say you'd step on me to get out of the play pen,
My thought would be that you always desired to win.

There's nothing wrong with the desire to win,
My brother did you forget you were born with a twin?
Branded identical from birth,
Until our feet would touch "Mother Earth."

Once upon a time we'd stick close like glue,
Yeah it was an honor to have a brother like you.

Lamont Bershawn

It was a joy to laugh, joke and play,
We were side by side each and every day.

Eventually, we'd part ways to do our own thing,
Our main focus was the bag... cha ching,
You'd have your friend and I'd have mine,
Certainly, no reason to have them intertwine.

You became infatuated with our martial arts instructor,
Many of the brothers knew that you became his sucker.
You wanted to be like him, dress like him and talk like him,
You became his shadow until your very own light was dim.

Wearing your Ashley Stewart jeans with the Jordan's I gave you,
The moment you almost cost me my life I knew I was through,
Pleasing mom I tried to remain cordial and forgiving,
Fuck this shit you have no regard whatsoever for the living.

I could care less about your sexual preference,
But every word spewing from your mouth made you reference,
Martial arts this, acting that, tournament this, his clothes that, one of his witches....
Huh? Made us think that you became one of his bitches.

Made me go back to that game of truth and dare,
You know the game that our eldest brother made us aware, When you were asked to kiss that dudes dick,
Without hesitation you did it like you were a chic.

You've told lies to the women I was serious about,
They believed you without a doubt,
You really thought you achieved your goal,
When in fact you only let me know that I was involved with a troll.

You keep telling folk that my books didn't sell,

When the truth of the matter is, they're doing quite well,
Your own women even wanted you to see,
After you fabricated your life you still couldn't be me.

Stealing from the Sweepstakes and the Doc more or less,
Does that 1982 Rolls really determine your height of success?
I'm not trying to humiliate you but you left me no choice,
You keep my name in your mouth like you're stealing my voice.

You've burned so many bridges you have no loyalty,
When the smoke clears, you're the one hollering, "Lamont, rescue me",
Your sister in law's the suicidal one,
And you're the convicted felon.

Now you lie on me until no end,
Face reality brother you'll never win,
No matter what you say or do,
I'll always be number one and you're number two.

Focus on the truth it will set you free,
Still all in all you'll never be me.
Woman after woman trying secure your insecurity,
Brother, the women that left you questioned your homosexuality!!

Now, I'll proceed on finishing my book,
Brothers warring on social media isn't a good look,
A writer from the heart, a Seer in my own right,
Constantly changing lives in order to bring people into the light.

When my life is over, I'll have no regrets,
I may not be drenched in diamonds, platinum or baguettes,
The wisdom that I share gives me a sense of peace,
As I continue my journey still looking towards the East.

- Lamont Bershawn {Original Piece}

THE INFANCY GOSPEL

Sunday, at 5:00a.m on February 11, 1973, I was born into the world. I had no clue what was going on nor the things I'd endure but whatever was going to happen I was certain that I was prepared for. Fifteen minutes later as my mother held me in her arms the nurse grabbed me while the doctor was telling my mother to push. I had no idea who that was that was coming outside of my mother, but his cry sounded familiar. I knew that he was someone special because we looked the same.

A very long time ago while being inside my mother's womb I envisioned a throne fit for a King. I stood up and began to inspect my surroundings. As I walked around, I saw many beings that I never knew, but as I passed them, they saluted me and stood at attention. I respectfully nodded my head to acknowledge everyone that I saw.

Out from the left a voice spoke to me {while kneeling} and said, "Hello Sir! They call me Adversary. I'm the one you've chosen to cause enough conflict during your earthly tenure in order to keep you on the right track." I responded, "Arise Adversary, this is a journey that neither you nor I will ever forget."

As I walked a little further to the right of me stepped out a set of triplets. They spoke in unison {while kneeling} and said, "Hello Sir! Our names are Trials, Tribulation and Temptation. We're the ones that you've chosen that will be in other people's paths that you'll come in contact with; the ones that will be there during your sleepless nights; the ones that will cause so much doubt." I responded, "Arise my set of triplets, this is a journey that neither you nor I will ever forget."

As I looked above my head, there were a set of twins hovering over my head. I asked, "Who might you be?" They said, "Your Excellency, we are Crown and Conqueror. We shall hover over you from now until eternity as you continue to rise above the feats of life."

Confused as all get out, I approached the throne and asked, "Where is the owner of this throne?"

In an instant, everyone knelt as the mirrors stood at attention speaking, "You are the Owner, Creator and King!"

POINT: While you yet were inside of the Goddess womb, you were the heir to the throne of life {glory}. You chose every battle/ fight, temptation/ trial and conflicting source. In other words, you knew them prior to your earthly existence.

Have you forgotten who you are? Have you really demoted your REAL name for a makeshift title?

Go back to the beginning and reclaim all that you've sold, was stolen or relinquished. It's all in the wrong hands/ possession if it's NOT in YOURS!! – Lamont Bershawn.

Growing up, we always admired and looked up to our oldest brother. He was almost three years older than us and the wonderful thing was that we all attended the same school. I can recall being in kindergarten when my mother would walk or drive us to school depending on the weather. My mother was very active in our school because she was a part of the Home and School Association, which was an organization that partnered with the school to make sure the students had a voice and was given a challenging curriculum and education.

My twin brother's name was Jerome and my oldest brother name was Kurt. Jerome and I were so close that it was a joy to see each other when we lined up against the wall to either go to the auditorium, lunch or recess. We'd always waive at each other and smile just to give each other a sense of comfort. Somehow, I'd always save a piece of my sandwich just to make sure Jerome had enough to eat, although mom had prepared the same thing for us to eat. Mom kept Jerome and I dressing like twins for years. I guess it was easier to buy two of the same things instead of looking for different attire. Whatever play or musical the school had we were going to be in it because mom kept us active in school functions to keep us busy. If it wasn't a school function then it was a church function. At one point it seemed that something was taking place in church every night.

Monday night- Usher meeting

Tuesday night- Choir rehearsal

Wednesday night- Bible study

Thursday night - Cleaning night

Friday night- Prayer and Tarrying service

Saturday night- Feeding the homeless

Sunday morning- Sunday school followed by all day worship

We attended a Pentecostal church so we didn't leave church until 5:00p.m.

Whenever Kurt, Jerome and I were home we'd always find something to do together like play video games, play word games, puzzles, cards and using educational tools like hooked on Phonics. The weekends we'd find joy going to our maternal grandparent's home because they had a swimming pool, pool table, hockey and ping pong table. They had so much to do over there but one of the greatest joys was playing with the dog and finding goodies in the bread box.

Kurt would always have a small paper bag filled with assorted chewy candy that he would get from the corner store. Jerome and I were too young to walk to the store by ourselves so Kurt would share a little of his candy with us. If we wanted a piece of gum, he'd bite a small piece and give a piece of a piece to each of us. Kurt's favorite piece of candy was between the Twizzlers or Reese's peanut butter cups.

My mother and grandmother kept us busy with activities and we also traveled to family reunions, funerals and weddings so that we'd get to know our relatives. It was always a joy to be around them because they always seemed to laugh, get along and were very hospitable. We didn't like visiting my dad's family often because they were strict and it really wasn't anything going on over there for little children. I mean, my cousin who was a year younger than me had a video game that we were able to play but it wasn't any sense for us taking our bicycles over there because we really didn't have anywhere to ride. I guess I really could understand a little realizing that my grandfather was already in his seventies and all they seemed to enjoy doing was going to church. The only time we really got the opportunity to see our cousins on my dad's side was either at a funeral, wedding or when we all went to New York for the week to visit my Aunt.

We had a pretty good life growing up. I mean we always had food on the table, clothes on our backs, a roof over our heads and we had each other. We respected each individual and never bothered to compare ourselves to anyone. We grew up in a middle-class neighborhood where everyone seemed to be family oriented and we got along well with everyone.

I remember one night my mother was cooking and we were sitting watching the news. I asked my mother to come and look at the news guy hairstyle and told her that's the way I'd like my hair to be. My mother said, "You want a part in your hair? Okay." The next morning, as my brothers and I were getting ready for school, my mother greased our hair with coconut oil and used her comb to part our hair. When we went to school the teachers looked and loved our hairstyle. I knew then it would be the style I'd keep for a long time. I was close to both of my brothers but closer to Jerome since we were twins. I still loved to be around Kurt because he always had a bag of goodies and kept me laughing. Kurt was a comedian at heart and he loved to make people laugh and I knew he had his own set of friends that were around his age, so he had to eventually entertain them too.

My parents became great friends with a few of our neighbors that had children Kurt's age and Kurt would go over their house to play games with them often. Jerome and I also had a few friends on the block that we'd visit. Whenever we'd play tackle football it would definitely been on our lawn. The older guys would play football at the dead-end street or in the cemetery because it was a wide opened grassy area. We had block parties where both ends of the street would be roped off and all cars would be off the street so games could be played, contests were given, all types of entertainment were there and everyone either had a grill cooking or people cooked in their homes and shared with everyone. It was like a blended community of unity.

My mother had a daycare for a few years before she decided to become a LPN {Licensed Practical Nurse} and decided to see if people were interested in going on a trip. Every year we'd take vacations to Florida to visit family or go to Disney, but some people never experienced getting out of the city either because they were short of finances or they never were introduced to vacationing. At a young age it never dawned on me that people could get so envious of you based on traveling. I spoke with a few of the neighborhood children and realized that they never got a chance to experience leaving the city because of their parents, so my mother had a meeting with the parents in the neighborhood and arranged a road trip to Jones Lake Camp located in North Carolina. When all was said and done my mother had five chaperones, two fifteen passenger vans, sixteen children a medic and police trooper. It was like a scene from the movie, "Bustin' Loose" featuring Cicely Tyson and Richard Pryor. The trip was amazingly fun and everyone seemed to have a blast.

We built campfires and told ghost stories, we toasted marshmallows and hotdogs, walked the nature trails, swam in the lake and also went fishing. We also were privileged to get a pass to White Lake where they had a huge game room, restaurants and a carnival on site. The water at White Lake was crystal clear and warm. My cousin Duke who was the park ranger also educated us about the animals in the area as well as the history of the parks. As the saying goes, "All good things must come to an end." We headed back home and the parents picked their children up. The response was extraordinary and a few parents wanted to know when the next trip was. This trip actually brought strangers together in the neighborhood that ended up building lifelong friendships. Somehow my mother knew how to make things happen with the knowledge she had and little to work with. A couple of weeks after the trip more of the children's parents began reaching out to my mother and somehow, we became good friends with the kids. We went to a fairly small church but by the time my mother finished speaking with the parents, we had new members. Anyone that knew us knew that church was a priority in our lives.

Here we are eight years old and Kurt is ten years old. Every summer our parents would take us to Disney World because for a few years our family reunion would be in Florida. The long drives would be fun because we got a chance to see things in a car that we couldn't see from an airplane. Heading to Florida we'd always stop at South of the Border which is actually the line between North and South Carolina. South of the Border was a tourist attraction because there were many shops that carried anything from fireworks to clothing and the "Big Sombrero" which was similar to the Eifel Tower that at the top you could see both North and South Carolina from an aerial view. When we got to Florida it was fun seeing relatives that we haven't seen in such a long time and taking part in family activities. We'd always stay at least two weeks, one week with family and the other week going to amusement parks, staying in luxurious villas and doing things educational.

The next school year would be challenging since my oldest brother would be attending another school and Jerome and I wouldn't be seeing him nor would he be walking with us to school. It was always a joy to see him when he came home though because he always found a way to bring home a small bag of assorted candy. We loved exercising, gymnastics, swimming, bowling and martial arts. My parents were on a bowling league so certain days they'd go bowling and it was a joy to watch them knock all the pins down or throw a strike. I guess anything was better than going to church listening to the boring and repetitive messages every week. One evening mom was cooking dinner and I remember dad running into the kitchen because mom got burnt while cooking chicken. I had no idea the handle on the pot broke and the hot grease spilled all over her arm. I remember my neighbor coming over and watching us while my dad took my mother to the hospital. It was hard sleeping that night because I wanted to make sure that my mother was going to be okay. When she came home, she had her arm bandaged but she looked at us and smiled, letting us know that she was going to be okay. We couldn't always get to my grandparent's house every week but when we did it was fun playing with the dog. We loved the dog so much that we wanted one at our house too. We asked if we could have a dog and my mother said sure but my dad said no, until we promised that we'd take care of it. We ran home from school every day for one week in hopes that the puppy would be there. We were exhausted from being disappointed that the puppy hadn't arrived yet until this one particular day we walk into the house and my mother is in the kitchen on the phone speaking with my grandmother. We walked into the dining room and saw this beautiful black puppy Doberman. He had huge paws, floppy ears and followed my mother around since he was used to her. The moment we saw him he began barking at us as we ran up to him and hugged him. We named him Zeus because we knew he was a true watch dog at heart. Zeus became familiar with us really quick as he found out that it was our job to walk and feed him. Zeus loved to play and sleep at the top of the stairs so he could watch who was coming through the front door and make sure we were protected upstairs. Zeus loved mom's cooking too, as we'd toss him a piece of chicken or put the broth over his regular food.

Mom would tell us how we were growing up. Mom said, "Kurt would get in trouble because he didn't have anyone to look up to, but Jerome and I learned from a few of Kurt's mistakes." I asked mom, "How did Jerome and I treat each other?" Mom responded, "Lamont, you'd always be the one to look out for Jerome. If I gave you both a sandwich, you'd break your sandwich in half just to make sure Jerome had enough to eat. Even when you both were in the play pen Jerome would use you as a step ladder to get out of the play pen. Jerome wanted all the attention, but you were my different child." "Your different child" I asked. Mom said, "Yes, anything that I seemed to be going through or dealing with you made sure that you were close by. It was like you felt my pain and was my protector. I know Kurt and Jerome wouldn't let anything happen to me neither, but it was evident with you."

Jerome began doing crazy things like sticking a toothpick in Zeus ass. Zeus never forgot it and would growl every time Jerome was near him. Jerome killed the parakeets by blowing a horn in their ear making them have a heart attack. I didn't understand what was going on with Jerome but Kurt saw something deeper than I did. Kurt is now twelve and Jerome and I are ten years old. We visited my cousin's house and played a game called truth or dare. Kurt dared Jerome to kiss John's penis and to everyone's surprise Jerome did it without hesitating. I asked Jerome "Is there something that you need to tell me or talk about?" Jerome just smiled and walked away. We went into the room and started lifting weights and practicing our martial art techniques. I was still shocked to what I witnessed Jerome do because I remember certain girls who liked Jerome. Jerome was the Captain of safety patrol and I became the Lieutenant a few weeks later. We were active participants in school functions and activities and very competitive when it came to school competitions. Actually, I have to give all the credit to my mother because she sold more than fifteen thousand dollars of candy and I won first place, which was a Colecovision game system. Jerome and I also were in the talent show wearing our karate uniforms and doing a few demonstrations. We knew this was our last year in this school so we had to leave a positive mark on all of our teachers and that we definitely did. Prior to the end of the school year my mother invited all of our teachers to the house for a "Thank You" dinner. They all were so appreciative but before they left my mother gave all of them a gift from Avon since she sold their products on the side.

Here it is a new school year and we're being bused from William Rowen Elementary School to LaBrum Middle School, a school approximately thirty minutes away from the house. It's a totally different environment and the teachers were attentive. Jerome and I were in different classes. Students were positioned in classes based on their academic skill, six-one was considered the smartest six-two was next and so on. I was in six-one and Jerome was in six-two but I really think they separated us to see how we'd get along and progress. Jerome and I joined the orchestra to learn a few instruments. Jerome played the Bass and I played the violin which meant we'd catch public transportation home together. I remember catching the bus and then catching the subway seeing these guys wearing red berets, red and white jackets and black pants calling themselves the "Guardian Angels." Their job was to assist police officers and to be a seen presence when police officers weren't around. When Jerome and I got home we began talking about becoming a member of the "Guardian Angels" when we got older. Jerome and I were picked on because we stood out or were different. We weren't with the fads that people were into we pretty much created our own style that people loved as others became jealous. We never thought that we were better than anyone else, well I didn't. I'd sit on the bus and help guys with their homework, meet people at lunch instead of going to recess I'd help them study for a test or figure out a better way for them to understand the subject. There were two teachers that stood out the most, both were math Professors. One of the teachers also worked at the Housing Police and had slick wavy hair like ours, so most of the students thought that he was our father. Mr. Cooper didn't tolerate any mess from anyone. The other teacher was the most gorgeous lady I'd ever put my eyes on and she was very classy. Mrs. Sturgis taught in such a way that she made sure that everyone passed her class and didn't let anyone slide through that wasn't able to grasp the formulas. She held tutorials before and after school just to make sure she set time aside for her students.

Jerome became close with Mr. Cooper because he always wanted to be a police officer and he thought Mr. Cooper could give him a few pointers. Jerome and I were on different committees helping setup at school events and functions. We joined the basketball team and although we didn't get a lot of playing time it was fun. One lasting memory that I'll always cherish is when the referee didn't show up for the game and my dad refereed the entire game, so neither team would forfeit.

My mother didn't keep us in the most expensive clothing because she didn't want our attention to become more about what we wore than what we learned. My mother would take us to the outlets to shop where the new clothes would be out prior to them hitting department stores. Now as for sneakers my mother wasn't buying expensive sneakers, so we wore a canvas sneaker, with three stripes and rubber curved front. Back in the day those sneakers were called, Bobo's. I was very creative so I remember drawing a swish on the side and writing Nike on the back of me and Jerome's sneakers. I recall during the class break one student looking at my sneakers asking, "Hey man, what kind of sneakers are they?" I replied, "These are the new Nike. Adidas and Nike were on the verge of merging until Adidas pulled out of the deal. Only one hundred pairs were released and my brother and I have two pair of the one hundred made." He responded, "Man, I really like them." I hated to lie but I didn't want to draw unnecessary attention to us. When Jerome and I got home my grandparents picked us up for the weekend.

The next morning, Jerome and I were outside riding our bikes and playing in the yard when he tripped over a branch and ripped his sneakers. My grandmother took us shopping and gave each of us one hundred dollars to buy a pair of sneakers. Jerome bought Magic Johnson sneaker and I bought a pair of Nike pump up basketball sneakers. We really enjoyed going to my Grandparents house because there was so much for us to do. At my Grandparents home there was a pool table, ping pong, air hockey table, hand bowling table, a swimming pool that went from 3 feet to 8 feet, a disc jockey set to make our own recordings and our personal Coca-Cola soda machine. When Jerome and I were there, we always seemed to have fun because we stayed busy doing educational studies or exhausting ourselves playing a few games.

The following week NASA was sending a shuttle into space and the entire school watched. On January 28, 1986, The Challenger space Shuttle that carried a seven-member crew, but first teacher, Christa McAuliffe, exploded in air. It's a day that I'll never forget because it traumatized everyone that witnessed history in the making.

In the end before we graduated Jerome and I were voted best dressed individuals. The saddest part of that year was that I knew one of my classmates had been abused for a number of years and didn't know how to handle his traumatic experiences, so he ended up killing his neighbor and going to prison at the age of fourteen.

Raised from a dead level:

There's a "Storm" for every dimension or level "God" elevates you to, it's called the test. Remember, in school in order to get to the next grade you had to pass a test to confirm your knowledge of what you've learned while you were on this level. Don't worry about pushing, just learn the signs. A storm never comes without a sign.

Everyone's not going to like or agree with everything you post or say. You have to expect opposition on every level of your life. It's not the people that are walking along side of you that will cause you to elevate, but it's the one's

(1) who think they know you

(2) the ones that are conflicting

(3) the one's that can't accept the elevation/ change in altitude

(4) the ones that have bruised knees for praying for so long, etc.

Many are walking on the same road, but are experiencing different storms. The "Hurricane" you've endured may very well be too much for the "Tornado" the next person endured; the "Tsunami" may be too much for you to handle and the "Earthquake" may have caused another to fall through the cracks.

The storm you're going through at this very moment is designed personally for you. You were chosen to go through the storm for the purpose of the outcome.

You may not remember, but YOU signed a contract with God prior to your existence. God placed you inside of a room with many symbols, just to show you the stages in which your travels must consist. God told you to everything there's a BEGINNING and an ENDING, then you came into existence.

POINT: {DON'T MISS THIS} We all experienced the lashes on a "cross" at one point or another because it happened at the crossroads of decision making. We carried the cross as a symbol of the death we've experienced during the storms of life which was the "BEGINNING" of WISDOM.

Once we can understand the levels of life, the symbols will begin to change or evolve just as the seasons.

Your lives will take on new meaning as you continue to breathe and transcend. The cross will remain as the many paths you'll discover and from that point you'll receive your "Ankh" which is the symbol of life but is the "ENDING" of one chapter into another realm.

RESPECT THE SIGNS THAT GOD HAVE GIVEN YOU!! - Lamont Bershawn.

The Liar That Lingers in the Closet

If you have ever belonged to a religious, military, racially deemed supreme, sorority or fraternal organization you've probably been told to ask yourself, "Am Eye my brother's keeper?" This question is given so that you understand the significance of a brotherhood or sisterhood relationship and what it means to be loyal. Most people really don't understand what it means to be loyal because along with loyalty comes respect. It's really impossible or hard for people to give to others what they refuse to give themselves.

When we became teenager's, it was still embedded in us that if we missed church on Sunday we couldn't go to the movies, bowling alley or to the skating rink. Kurt, Jerome and I were always active in some form of martial art. Jerome and I started out with Tae Kwon Do at an early age and my father was teaching Kurt Judo.

In March of 1985, Kurt came home one evening with two other guys that went to school with him. One was an artist and the other was a dancer. Kurt introduced them to the family as Rob and Frank. Rob and Frank saw Jerome and myself practicing Karate and invited us to take part in their class. They did an amazing demonstration and we couldn't wait to join. Kurt, Jerome and I went to their next martial arts class and we were dedicated from that point on. Our martial arts instructor was also an Opera singer and an actor. His name was Sifu Hulk because he actually resembled the green muscular guy. Jerome was fascinated with Sifu to say the least that Jerome wanted to look like Sifu, dress like Sifu and talk like Sifu. I must be honest and say that under Sifu direction we entered a lot of tournaments and learned to properly defend ourselves, although it seemed better to avoid or walk away from fights. We knew our skill even though the opponent

The Liar That Lingers in the Closet

didn't and although no one is underestimated when it comes to battle, both parties could leave unharmed. Bruce Lee said it best, "Learn to master the art of fighting without fighting."

All of Sifu students during this era considered each other brothers. Beyond what we were taught at home, Sifu wanted to always see our report cards and taught us to always be there for each other. It was awesome because now I had another set of brothers that I could reach out to besides Jerome and Kurt. Any problem we had with each other was always talked about and handled in the class amongst ourselves. It was evident a few years later that Jerome had become "The teacher's pet" because he had a key to Sifu apartment and was his "watch dog" meaning he was the lookout person that would tell Sifu when his main chic was on the way. Jerome received gifts from Sifu Hulk like a pair of black jeans by Ashley Stewart, which more than likely was a pair of one of his chic jeans but because they were a gift, Jerome wore them with pride.

Deep down within I knew something wasn't right with their close net relationship and very disturbing that I and other brothers decided to disconnect from Sifu Hulk's class. This is when Jerome labeled himself Sifu number one student and his mentality totally changed towards everyone. I didn't know how far Jerome allowed to go to his head until we went to school and he began telling people that {we} were in the movie, "Coming to America" featuring Eddie Murphy and Arsenio Hall. People asked him, "What did you do in the movie?" Jerome replied, "We did the stick fighting for Eddie and Arsenio and we were extras in the airport scene." Jerome felt comfortable including me in his lie so he wouldn't look stupid by himself when people actually saw the movie and saw other people actually doing their stick fighting.

Here it is, we just moved into a new home in the suburbs and transferred from George Washington High School now attending Cheltenham High School and Jerome wants to draw attention towards us. I mean we're already going to receive attention because we're twins, but I guess Jerome felt the need to feel like a child celebrity. I really didn't think it was a big deal because quite a few celebrity children attended the school. It wasn't a big deal until the movie broke the box office record in the first week, then I thought, "People went out to see the movie and we're going to be scolded by classmates for Jerome's lie." The funny thing is Jerome and I were walking the hall together and one of his classmates yelled down the hall {getting everyone's attention} "Yo Jerome, I saw you guys in Coming to America." I thought to myself, "Either this guy is setting us up, on drugs or senile."

Word got around school that we were a couple of actors. One of the math teachers had a side business of photography and he offered to take our pictures and make us a portfolio. He actually blew one of the photos up and gave it to our mother. The math teacher was also a great marketer of his business, so he allowed us to select our favorite single headshot picture each and he made twenty copies of each photo. He told us to take them to school and show a few people the shots. Little did we know but the ladies loved the photos and asked us to order some and autograph them. Jerome and I autographed the ones we had and told them how much the other pictures would cost to order. I felt bad because we weren't in "Coming to America" but I never acknowledged or answered any questions about that when asked, so people would say, "He's being humble and modest."

A door opened up from that because Jerome and I were actually playing prisoners in a movie named "Condition Red" featuring James Russo. I felt better now that we were actually in a movie where our names could be seen in the credits at the end of the movie. Still in school, Jerome was professing the continued lie about "Coming to America." I found out it was actually the lie that Sifu told people and Jerome adopted the same lie to tell his friends.

Here it is February 1991 and we just had our eighteenth birthday. We only had four months until high school graduation. Jerome and I went to my grandparent's house to relax and the Army recruiter contacted us to meet him at his office. When we arrived at his office, he took us to take the ASVAB {Armed Services Vocational Aptitude Battery} test. We passed the test and Jerome was excited about enlisting, but I was more interested in going into the Air Force since that's where my father joined.

Nevertheless, we went to the MEPS {Military Entrance Processing Station} and went through a series of tests and a physical. When it was time to sign on the dotted line Jerome didn't hesitate to sign and I refused to sign. When we arrived home, Jerome told our mother that he signed up to join the Army. She was happy for him until she found out that I refused to sign up. My mother began to cry because she didn't want him to join the military alone. She looked at me and said, "Can you please reconsider and sign up. I'd feel better knowing that someone is over there watching him." I responded, "God got him and god don't need my help watching out for Jerome."

This is when I knew my mother's faith waivered when it came to that religious deity. I knew deep down within my spirit the entire religious doctrine was bullshit. I hated to see my mother cry and worry so the next day I reluctantly signed up to join the Army under the "buddy system" which meant that Jerome and I wouldn't be separated.

In 1997, when Eye joined the Masonic Organization there were two requirements. The first requirement was that Eye had to believe in a "Supreme" being, the second required two Masons had to vouch for my character and bring me in. One of the brother's that brought me in was my biological brother who joined two years prior to me and the other was my play Uncle who at the time was the Past Most Excellent Grand High Priest. Eye should have known there was a weakness in the brotherhood being as though my biological brother was still active and wasn't kicked out because he seemed to always get in some sort of trouble. Eye gave the Masons the benefit of doubt that maybe they could turn his life around for the better.

During the time my group had to show proficiency in front of other brothers to determine whether we could cross over or repeat the class. Eye was the President of my class, so Eye made the commitment to make sure we knew our lines and were sharp using signals and motions. Whenever one of the brothers stumbled Eye was there to make sure they'd remember their part. Eye guess this was the beginning of letting the other brother's see that Eye understood what it meant to have my brother's back. Whenever we went to lodge meetings or met up with other members of different fraternities someone would ask me the question, "Am Eye my brother's keeper?" Eye could strongly answer, "Eye'm."

Still being active with the Masonic Organization Eye moved to Florida in 1998. Eye had family member's there and a few friends. Jerome's best friend lived there and he too was a Mason. Actually, he was the President of the line when Jerome crossed over. Ron was a family man and was also in the military. His children called me Uncle and they treated me like family. Ron and Jerome were close and would do anything for each other. Eye mean at least Ron would always do things like invite Jerome to sporting events, birthday parties at their home, special occasions at his wife's job, etc. Eye guess he tried to get Jerome to meet someone special and settle down with a good woman, but Jerome had other things on his mind.

Okay, let's take a step back!

A few years into being a Mason Eye'd go to the cabarets, the parades and some of the functions or fundraisers at some of the brother's homes. You know Eye just wanted to see who'd show up at times and see what was so special about them. All Eye'll say is they knew how to throw a successful event.

Jerome asked me to ride with him one evening to one of the Masonic events, where Eye'd meet Ron and his wife. Ron was a determined brother. Eye mean just his conversation alone was about creating some form of business. He said that his wife had her degree and was a registered nurse, so he knew that he had to get on the ball because he'd soon be discharging from the Navy. Eye could tell that Jerome wasn't paying much attention to Ron because he was trying to talk to every woman that passed by him. We stayed a few hours and then Jerome and Eye left. When we got in the car Eye told Jerome that he should keep Ron as a friend. One thing Eye knew is that good friends pushed their true friends to desire to achieve more and have a better life. Jerome didn't want good friends; he desired those friends that would constantly place him on a pedestal and boost his ego. My guess is he got that from our dad.

One evening Jerome wrecked his car, but he wasn't hurt. His car only had liability so he was without a car. Eye wasn't one to party or go out many places so Eye'd allow Jerome to drive my car. Jerome and Eye were fairly close until Eye realized that he had no regard for my things and he was just a careless person. When he burned out my clutch to my vehicle and refused to pay a portion of it is when Eye decided to limit his use of my belongings. This would mean that if he had a date either Eye had to take him, he had to catch the bus or find transportation. We'd often double date going to dinner or the movies. It seemed that every time things seemed to be going well something would happen that cause Jerome and Eye to come at odds end. Jerome would have these women that would tell him, "Your brother looks better than you." Eye guess it gave him a complex and that these women would rather date me than him. Oddly enough Jerome began disliking and hating me. Things began getting ugly to the point Eye had to distance myself away from him, so that women he'd begin dating wouldn't even know he had a twin. He'd tell them he had a brother, but not a twin and to make matters worse he'd degrade me so if they ever met me, they'd already have a negative mindset about me. Eye had to remember what my mother would always tell me about how Jerome would act as a baby. Eye know this is why Eye'd forgive him so many times because Eye'm the older brother. Throughout our childhood, even up to that point if the question was asked, "Am Eye my brother's keeper?" My answer would have been "Yes."

Ron was going to sea on his last tour before his contract was up. He told Jerome that he'd be relocating to Florida and that he'd keep him posted. Ron asked Jerome to look out for his wife and children while he was away at sea. Meanwhile, the company Eye was working for had an opening in Florida. Two thoughts crossed my mind. First, Eye needed to put some distance between me and Jerome in order to have a fresh start. Prior to me heading out to Florida Eye had to briefly stop by my parent's other home to get some of my things. When Eye pulled up to the house the lights were on. This was strange to me because no one was occupying the house at this time, so Eye pulled around back and a black car was parked directly behind the house. As Eye got out of the car and proceeded to enter the back door, it opens. Walking out the back door was Jerome and Ron's wife. Ron's wife had the look on her face as if she saw a ghost. Eye spoke to the both of them and asked Jerome, "Why are you and Ron's wife over here alone?" Jerome responded, "We had to go over a few things." Eye let that go because Eye knew Jerome was lying.

When Eye arrived to Florida Eye was on a mission. Eye mean Eye was single, didn't have any children, had a good job and was saving money. Eye began networking, working another job, moved into my own place and really didn't have much time to visit family. Eye went to the Post Office to send a package to my mother and who did Eye run into? Yep, Eye ran into Ron. Ron looked at me and said, "Eye know this isn't my brother all the way from the City of Brotherly Love! We shook hands and greeted each other with a brotherly hug. We asked about each other's family. Then he said, "Tina and the kids are outside in the truck. We're on our way to dinner. Won't you come along?" Eye really didn't want to go because Eye didn't want his wife to get nervous wondering if Eye'd say anything to Ron and also because Eye knew about his wife's infidelity and didn't mention it. Eye was caught between a rock and a hard place.

Eye mean being a twin isn't always as much fun as it's portrayed or people think. People used to always approach us saying, "Eye wish Eye had a twin." Being a twin would be great if both were positive thinking individuals, be great for Hollywood and also great for being a stunt double.

Here Eye'm sitting in the presence of my Masonic brother with his family acting as if nothing happened between his wife and Jerome. Is this what a brotherhood consisted of? It wasn't in my eyes. Dinner was great as Eye was able to escape the midst without anyone picking up that my spirit was vexed. Eye went home and couldn't wait to pick up the Bible to see if Eye could find scripture that would validate Jerome's actions. The closest thing Eye could come up with was Deuteronomy 25:5, "If brothers are living together and one of them dies without a son, his widow must not marry outside the family. Her husband's brother shall take her and marry her and fulfill the duty of a brother-in-law to her." {New International Version}. Well, they weren't real brothers and neither of them was dead, so this was considered adultery.

The following weekend Ron asked me to ride with him a few places. We went to the flea market, the PX {Post Exchange} where military people shopped for goods, the auto parts store and grabbed a bite to eat. Ron began asking how Jerome was doing, but Eye did my best to keep every answer pertaining to Jerome extremely short. Ron made the statement, "Eye hope Jerome learned his lesson about chasing pussy." Eye asked Ron, "Why what happened?" Ron said, "Eye had to save his ass on one occasion when a dude caught him in bed with his children's mother. He met this chic at one of our cabarets that Eye told him not to fuck with because she's flaming. He left with her and before Eye could get out the door they were gone. Eye called him several times leaving messages but Jerome never answered. Eye guess he thought that Eye was "cock blocking." When Eye got hold of Jerome the next day, he told me that he fucked her, but he used protection. Now, me knowing Jerome he didn't like using condoms, but maybe he listened to me. Jerome said, "We had sex, she showered and left. Thirty minutes later she called and said that she was HIV positive." Jerome was so scared that he told me that all he could do was go home and hold his daughter in his arms.

Eye was speechless when Ron mentioned these things to me. Now Eye knew there was no way Eye was going to continue a conversation about Jerome. Ron dropped me off and asked me to meet him at his house tomorrow afternoon because Tina was meeting up with her sorority sisters and Eye could potentially meet a friend there. Eye was at their home the next afternoon and we went to the DST {Delta Sigma Theta} function. Eye met a young lady there named Bria. Bria and Eye exchanged information and began dating. This did two things; it kept me from always hanging at Ron's and kept me focused on my relationship with Bria. We had a lot of fun because we enjoyed doing pretty much the same things. Eye helped her with her Spanish class and she was an awesome cook. She was the type of woman that knew how to treat a man. Whenever Eye got off work went home to shower Eye knew dinner would be waiting when Eye arrived. We exchanged keys to each other's place, that's how serious we became. Ron also gave me a key for emergency purposes, but Eye never used it.

Eye never wanted to plant a negative seed in anyone's mind, especially if it could be prevented. Eye've learned that being a "brother's keeper" is extremely hard work, especially if you felt the need to cover or protect one due to their personal and foolish decisions. Jerome always looked at me as the bad guy though and had his constituents believing him, but Eye knew the truth. The difference between he and Eye is that he'll create lies to destroy a person's character but Eye'll tell the truth and present evidence.

"One of the MOST DANGEROUS people you'll come across in your life is a habitual liar. They're so hurt to the point they lose their true identity trying their best to be someone they're incapable of being.

Most of them are bipolar. They're so envious of you that they begin creating shit in their own minds just to think on your level.

The sad part of it is they begin believing their own lies and get viciously upset when people don't go along with them. Real men take care of and claim ALL of their children, their responsibilities and try to live a productive life!" - Lamont Bershawn.

It never really dawned on me that people would consider twins alike or similar in every way possible. Eye mean we're still individuals and have different minds. Eye'm assuming that people think this way because twins usually are much closer to each other and usually dress alike. We don't share a brain nor do we like the same types of things.

"This is going to HELP somebody:

Just because things look alike or similar don't mean they have the same qualities.

A Chrysler 300 only looks like a Bentley from a distance, but once they're side by side they look NOTHING alike.

Most people won't qualify for the Bentley so they'll settle for the Chrysler 300.

POINT: NEVER settle for LESS than what's desired. You're setting yourself up for a lifetime of misery!!" - Lamont Bershawn.

Here Eye am in Florida living on my own, happy and free from all of the drama and mess especially involving Jerome. Things between Bria and Eye just fell off, but we remained good friends. Eye knew in a couple of months our family reunion would take place here in Florida so Eye was preparing to see relatives that Eye hadn't seen in quite a while. A few weeks prior Eye had to drive back up north to gather a few things. When Eye arrived Jerome was out of town and come to find out that one of my exes was at my parent's house. She was fresh out of the military {so you'd think she'd either have a place to stay or a few dollars saved up}. This young lady was very attractive but she was scorned deep down within. Eye asked my mother, "Why is she staying here? Don't her mother still live in town?" My mother is a very giving person and opens her heart to the world. Well, come to find out Donna {my ex} mother was evicted from her home and had to move with her brother. Eye knew Donna was still very much in love with me, but in my eyes, she was definitely my past.

When Eye was heading back to Florida she asked if she could tag along just to keep me company for the thirteen-hour ride. Eye allowed her to ride with me, after Eye had an extensive conversation with my mother. When we arrived at my place in Florida, we unpacked the car Eye showed her to her room and we settled in. The next morning, Eye had to leave for work and she had breakfast on the stove. She stayed up all night reorganizing my cabinets as if she was going to be there for a minute. Eye made her feel welcomed, took her out to Jazz night, movies and shopping. Eye finally asked her, "You mean to tell me there isn't anyone special in your life?" She responded, "Yes, he's a Mason like you, but you know you'll always be my first true love." As we were having a conversation about him, he calls her phone. She was reluctant on answering the call, but Eye assured her that she could answer the call there's nothing going on between us. The guy she was dating was still in the military but he had no real idea where Donna was. Here Eye'm once again thinking, "Am Eye my brother's keeper?" Eye told Donna that she had my blessings in marrying or proceeding with another man because in my eyes as well as my heart the flames went out way before graduating high school. A few days later Eye dropped Donna off at the bus station and she departed with tears in her eyes. A few months later Donna was married. Man, this was a relief Eye thought as if she'd live a happy life with her husband.

Everything was going well and approximately one year later, mom called me telling me that Donna and her husband wanted to know if it was okay to stay with them until they found a place to live? Of course, mom said it was okay. Who brings their husband to stay with their ex-boyfriend parents? Now it was my mother's turn to be the "keeper." Eye assume that Donna never told her husband who this nice lady was because she began calling Jerome her brother, my eldest brother Kurt her brother and Eye was Uncle to her newborn. Yes, she had a child to presumably fill the void she felt from an abandoned relationship with her mother and never knowing her father. Donna and Eye were still pretty much okay with each other and Eye was glad she was married, although Eye knew she didn't marry this guy for love but stability. Donna and Eye had conversations about overcoming her hurt. She began to despise her mother, cuss out her sister because every time she turned around her sister kept having babies that she couldn't support. Donna was really on edge and Eye thought she was going to have a nervous breakdown, a heart attack or commit suicide. It got to the point that we'd talk regularly. She was very active in her church as a "greeter" and participated in other auxiliaries in the church.

Well, Donna always liked the attention of others because she grew up not getting much attention at all. Donna was pretty much the neglected one and her mother would call her, "Cow." Eye thought, "What a fucking insult." Eye thought Donna and Eye were pretty cordial until word got back to me that Donna started speaking about my family in such a negative way. Eye had to ask myself, "Is this the same young lady that my Grandmother had to explain how to get a bath as an adult?" "Is this the same young lady that always wanted to spend time at my home?" "Is this the same young lady that wanted to marry me because she was in love with me?" "Is this the same young lady that waited until she was twenty-two to give me her virginity?" "Is this the same young lady that Eye took out of town, bought expensive jewelry for and gave a surprise party for inviting all of her friends?" Eye was taken back for a moment, and then Eye realized it is the same woman that desired to be with me but became scorned when she wasn't my choice. Eye guess she had the right to be mad or upset with me because she never had a man that would treat her as well as Eye did. Linda Creed said it best, "The greatest love of all is the love that Eye have for me."

Jerome heard that Donna was upset and had something against me, so he decided to get in contact with her in order to play on her intelligence. It was just another person that he could get on his team that despised me. Eye began to ask the question, "Why is it so hard for a person to leave well enough alone and create a productive life for themselves, instead of trying to degrade another?" Eye had to dissect this question in order for me to make sense of it. You see it's easy for me to cut, dismember or disconnect myself from anyone that's not beneficial for where Eye'm headed.

LISTEN UP:

People are going to talk about you, degrade you, dislike you, lie on you, steal from you but MOST of all fear YOU; yet they still want to remain attached to you.

"Mutha Fukkas" that constantly want to talk shit about you really desire to be like you but are intimidated by everything you stand for. These are the same "b.i.t.c.h n.i.g.g.a.s" that build themselves up with lies in order to place themselves on a makeshift pedestal.

Notice there's a (.) after each letter which let you know there's a deeper meaning to the word given. A "b.i.t.c.h" is nothing more than a Broke{n} or Bitter Individual Trying to Cause Havoc and "n.i.g.g.a.s" are Negative Ignorant Guy or Girl After Something.

Be watchful because they'll have you be-LIE-ving their bullshit when in fact the ONLY thing they have going for themselves is gossiping, deceiving, lying, and perpetrating. They're nothing more than leeches trying to suck every ounce of opportunity from you.

Kings and Queens don't allow yourselves to get sidetracked or lose focus. Just KNOW that YOU'RE the ones that are on the correct path. The ones that are talking the MOST shit are the ones that NEED to reevaluate their lives because their compass has malfunctioned.

"Always keep in mind; a peasant will do whatever it will take to conquer anyone's throne!" - Lamont Bershawn.

  Even though Jerome despised me and was building a team full of haters, Eye still loved him because he was my brother. Eye didn't trust him as much but Eye'd give him the benefit of doubt for my mother's sake. Jerome began dealing with a new young lady and he seemed to be head over heels for her. The first thing that came to my mind was maybe she'd make him change his ways for the better. Come to find out, this chic was Jerome's best friend girlfriend and she's more vindictive than he is. This was a code breaker, especially dealing with your best friend's lady. This meant there wasn't any loyalty and could end up in a real bad situation. Funny thing is that evening Jerome's best friend called me and said something didn't seem right with his lady actions. Eye didn't want to tell him that she was involved with Jerome; Eye wanted Jerome to be a man and get things straight with his best friend.

"Am Eye my brother's keeper?" "Yes, Eye'm." Eye guess by now some of you are asking, "Why?" It's because Jerome seemed to be doing dumb shit without thinking and eye didn't want my brother dead, but he surely wasn't making things easy. If Eye didn't care Eye wouldn't have covered his ass on numerous occasions. It got to the point that Eye felt the need to protect him and he would think that Eye had nothing better to do than follow him. This brought me back to remembering the time my mother asked Jerome and Eye to go to church with her. During the service the visiting preacher stopped her sermon and pointed into the congregation towards Jerome. She said, "Son, there's a bullet with your name on it." She asked both of us to come up for prayer. She looked at me and said, "Eye'm going to anoint your head, your feet and your hands that wherever he goes you won't. You're a preacher and God is going to draw so many to you." She looked at Jerome and said, "The only reason you're alive is because your brother has been around as your protector when somebody desired to kill you." She looked at my mother and said, "God's going to throw Jerome in jail to get his attention, but don't be upset because it's for his own good." Eye was still very much active in the church at this time and knew what my spirit was feeling but Eye couldn't allow Jerome to get in deep trouble because he had a daughter to look after.

"When someone is trying their best to "Kick you under the bus", it's only because they don't realize they're already so far under the bus drenched with oil. It's the oil that has blocked their view of things and is beginning to cause them to suffocate. It's because of you having your hand held out to help them that making it hard for

them to accept because of their own guilt. Distressed situations call for desperate measures!!" -

POINT: *Be careful/ mindful of the bridges you PERSONALLY burn; YOU never know when YOU just may have to cross that bridge again! - Lamont Bershawn.*

Eye began feeling like we were in a movie because we weren't raised by our parents to hate or dislike each other. Eye felt like we were in "Money Train", Jerome was Woody Harrelson and Eye was Wesley Snipes. The only difference was they were play brothers and we weren't. In the movie Woody Harrelson always seemed to get himself in trouble because he had a serious gambling addiction and Wesley Snipes would always be there as his protector as well as pull him out of trouble. When a person is addicted to anything, it becomes part of who they are and therefore a habit. This was just one thing among many that set Jerome and Eye a part. Eye was afraid that one day it would cost some of our mutual and true friends to see us as being the same because we're twins. One of my greatest decisions was to get away as far as possible from Jerome because he was a time bomb waiting to explode and it was only a matter of time. Eye received a phone call from a mutual friend of ours. He said, "Eye must apologize to you." Eye responded, "For what?" He began to say, "Just because you're a twin Eye considered the both of you identical in every way, but Eye've come to realize that Jerome is a habitual liar." All Eye could do was feel a sense of relief that someone finally figured it out. Eye accepted his apology and then he began going in detail of some of the lies Jerome told him. To be honest Eye really didn't care about listening, Eye was more pleased with the fact he found out that Jerome and Eye were totally different individuals. It seemed that the more distance Eye placed between the two of us the more people that knew us could see the truth. Then it hit me, "people could never really tell us a part so we both received the blame of doing dumb shit." A few months had gone by and it was around Christmas time.

The Liar That Lingers in the Closet

Eye had to mail off a few things and some Eye had to drop off at United Parcel Service {UPS}. When Eye pulled up to the UPS store, Eye began filling out the information on the cards and boxes. On this particular day the weather was pretty nice. As Eye'm sitting in the car Eye could see a young lady to the left of the car just staring at me. When Eye looked up, she was looking directly at me so Eye paused from writing. Eye lowered my window to see if she was okay. In essence Eye really wanted to know what she was staring so hard for. She approached the car and asked, "Are you from Philadelphia?" Well, being as though Eye was from Philadelphia but sitting in a parking lot in Georgia sparked my interest. Eye said, "Yes, do you know me from somewhere?" She asked, "Do you have a daughter?" Eye said, "No, but my brother has a daughter." She began describing my house as if she definitely been there before. Eye said, "You thought Eye was Jerome." She responded, "When you began to speak Eye realized that you weren't Jerome because he's an arrogant, conniving, effeminate, punk ass liar." All Eye could do was say, "wow." Eye had to ask her, "What did he do to you?" It seemed as if she had a shopping list of things to say but she just said, "He depicts himself of way more than what he really is." Eye smiled and said, "Yep, that's Jerome." She began tot also say, "Eye never met you because Jerome never wanted me to meet you. Eye guess not because for one you look much better than he does {although you guys are twins} and he destroys your character to make people prejudge you prior to them actually meeting you." My heart was saddened to the fact that Jerome would speak so negatively of me but glad that another person realized who he really was. Eye realized that Jerome {being my brother} was more deadly and dangerous than Eye thought.

"When a person will do just about anything {lie, fabricate, mislead} to assassinate a person's character based on their reality it just means it's hard for that individual to accept self. They must now create an alias in which would redirect them from looking at the Medusa of self." - Lamont Bershawn.

It has always been in my heart to allow people to see or view an individual from their own perception instead of planting any seeds. The way Eye perceive someone or connect with them may not be the way another person views them, so it's best to just let them judge a person's character by their personal experience.

Eye had my own place in Florida and Jerome wanted to visit. Eye was reluctant at first but after talking it over with my mother Eye allowed him to stay with me for a week. The first few days went well probably because Eye was working nights and would drop Jerome off at my grandparents {Eye just didn't trust him being in my home all alone}. Eye knew Jerome was a jealous and envious individual yet Eye still gave him the benefit that maybe he changed his ways. While he was there, he met a young lady and she had a girlfriend that he suggested that Eye meet. We decided to go to dinner at Famous Amos one evening, double dating and he began to open his mouth building himself up as if he was Sean "Puffy" Combs or the Sultan of Brunei. Jerome even lied to these women and told them the song they were listening to on the cd was us. They asked him to sing along with it and boy did he sound bad. Eye'll never forget it because he told them that Eye sang the other part of the song. Eye just smiled and closed my eyes because Eye wasn't going to involve myself or engage in his foolishness. Eye really wasn't hungry but it was an open door to break the ice just to see where Jerome's head was. Well, Eye didn't go along with the lies Jerome was telling these women so he decided to try to make me look crazy in front of them. Eye decided to get up and walk away because Eye didn't want to cause a scene nor did Eye desire to make Jerome look like the ass he really was. Little did Jerome know these women were already on to him and his fabricated lifestyle. Well, Eye did my best trying to be cordial and fix whatever issues he carried in his heart concerning me. This was the beginning of me breaking the mold of me being my brother's keeper anymore. It seemed that every woman he began dealing with would see who Jerome really was. Even to this day Jerome no longer let women know he has a twin brother. The woman he was madly in love with destroyed him and gave him a complex concerning me. Eye was the brother that always had his back even when they said Eye was the "better looking" twin. Eye'd always come back and say that we're identical. Eye wasn't the one being labeled the conceited one, the habitual liar, the homosexual {although only a few people knew Jerome liked going into gay clubs and only a few people saw Jerome kiss a man on his penis}, yes it shocked the hell out of me.

Eye asked Jerome was he gay but he always shunned the question. Eye just knew he did a lot of things that straight men would never think of. Eye mean what man wore Ashley Stewart jeans? This was a woman's store. He followed so closely behind our martial arts instructor to the point he was known as his shadow. When the martial arts instructor was caught hugged up with a man in a vehicle Eye knew it was the end of the road with me going to class. Eye mean the martial arts instructor would always have different women over his house daily during class but Eye found out it was all a front. Eye guess some men want people to think they're straight the reason they seem to always have different women around or seek different women out, but they would rather be cuddled up next to a man. No wonder Jerome and our martial arts instructor was so close and understood each other. Then it dawned on me that Jerome could be a bisexual pedophile. Eye'm saying pedophile because Jerome also was propositioning his daughter's girlfriends who were under the age fourteen.

The time was now for me to clean the slate and protect my reputation from Jerome's bitterness, false accusations and lies. Eye was no longer going to leave well enough alone or be passive waiting for some "Lord" to handle it. Eye was no longer going to stand by and allow his lies to destroy another person. Jerome already got his best friend kicked out of the police academy two weeks prior to graduation, yet Jerome didn't mind using his best friend's badge number to get into the movie theater free. Jerome also lied to get me locked up for fourteen hours. Jerome made a negative statement that could have given someone life in prison and last but not least Jerome blackballed a friend by calling the police acting like he was a detective to get him three years behind bars. Yes, Eye had to distance myself because Eye knew doing this type of stuff would get him a free pass to the cemetery. It was time for me to accept our differences and stop making excuses as if everything about us was identical.

Often times we get so caught up trying to be like another person or be on one accord that we get side swiped into the waves and get swept under the currents.

We all endure in what's known as "Truth." There's {My, Our or Their} truth. My truth is the manifestation of my life which became a reality of what Eye was born with, when Eye poured into me. Your truth is what manifests in your life and Our truth is when we meet on one accord, pouring/ investing into us to make things happen.

It's impossible for something to come out, if it was never placed within to begin with.

We as individuals and collective participants must direct our "Energy" {Inner- "G"} in positive places.

"G" {the All- seeing Eye} or secret order which explains the geometrically maneuvering of greatness!!

The {Inner-" G"} is nothing more than the "God" within you. Look at it like this: Many people talk about faith, but faith only moves with "Energy" - the energy of the mind/ thought.

You still ultimately must have the physical "Energy" to move and the spiritual {Inner-" G"} to make it come to pass!!

What's your {Inner- "G"} directed towards? - Lamont Bershawn.

Wait! Allow me to take a few steps back to elaborate on the two times Eye've been arrested. The first time was Mother's Day weekend, 1998. My mother was in Florida visiting my grandmother. Jerome and Eye decided that we'd drive down to also spend the holiday with them. Friday evening Jerome and Eye got into an argument over something trivial, but he took it to a different level. This is when

Eye really figured out that he hated me to the point he wanted me dead or he was really mentally disturbed. Eye was in the den talking on the phone with my mother and she asked, "When are we leaving to head to Florida?" Jerome walks in the room to where Eye was standing and said, "Eye should blow your brains out." He left the room and headed upstairs, meanwhile Eye told my mother that Eye'd call her back. Eye wasn't concerned with Jerome getting a firearm from upstairs because my dad had all of his weapons locked up in a safe place and mine was unloaded in a lock safe in the trunk of my car. What Jerome did while being upstairs surprised me to a degree but then again Eye should have known he was up to no good. Eye was still in the den when Eye saw a beam of light flash across the backdoor's window, so Eye opened the back door to see what the beam of light was. As soon as Eye opened the door there were five police officers in my driveway with their guns drawn. Eye wasn't nervous or scared because Eye wasn't about to make any sudden moves or give them a reason to shoot. One of the officers said, "Come outside with your hands up." Eye let them know that Eye wasn't armed and Eye came outside and lay on the ground with my arms stretched out. One of the officers came and handcuffed me. As soon as Eye got handcuffed Jerome bursts outside and begins telling the police that Eye threatened to blow his brains out and that my gun was in the trunk of my car. Eye didn't say a word as Eye looked at Jerome in disgust knowing that he'd go to the extreme to blatantly lie on me. The officer got the keys to my car, opened the trunk and retrieved the case where my gun was. Eye arrived to the police station and was being processed in. When the detective looked at me as he was fingerprinting me, he said, "Eye'm sure of one thing?" Eye responded, "What's that?" He said, "Eye can tell that your brother is a fucking liar."

For a moment there was a sigh of relief, but Eye was still being processed. Fourteen hours later Eye went before the judge and paid my own bail. My eldest brother Kurt picked me up and Eye told him what happened. A week later Eye went to court with my mother and Uncle Tom by my side. When we arrived at court Jerome was sitting with a few police officers busting it up as if he was an officer himself. The judge dismissed all charges and the prosecutor told me that Eye was free to pick up my firearm at the police station next door. When Eye got to the police station to pick up and sign for my weapon the Captain said, "Eye'm sorry that you had to go through this."

When Eye got in the car with my mother and Uncle my mouth was open but my spirit was speaking, "Jerome's going to tell a lie on someone one day to the point it's going to cost them their life or freedom." Eye was focused more than ever to get away from this dude because wasn't anything good or positive happening for him and he was like a blazing tornado without a conscience.

In 1999, Eye moved to Florida because my job had a position opening and it would be a great distant away from the unnecessary drama that Eye was being pulled into. Finally, being free and able to advance my life into a new and better direction Eye began applying to explore different careers in the workforce. Eye was doing extremely well.

In Dec. 2002, Eye just arrived to work and Eye received a call from Jerome. Jerome and Eye were very cordial up to this point because Eye really didn't trust him. Eye was a little nervous for a few reasons one was because it was still early in the morning and two, he never really had anything good or positive to say. Let's just say Jerome loved to be the "bearer of bad news." Eye said, "What's up Jerome?" He asked, "Are you sitting down?" At that point Eye knew it wasn't good, especially for him to make the attempt to give me bad or upsetting news. Eye responded, "Yes, Eye'm sitting down. What's up?" "Kurt was just framed for murder. The police just picked him up from his home and are taking him in for questioning. It's already on the internet." Eye immediately got off the phone and pulled up the information on the internet. You know Eye didn't trust anything Jerome said, so Eye had to validate the information. My heart seemed to drop to the bottom of my feet as Eye couldn't imagine what my parents were feeling. Eye made arrangements to take a leave of absence to be closer to my family during this time of emergency. Jerome was in touch with a mutual friend of ours that wanted to move up north. He and

Jerome had an agreement, so Rick would end up helping me drive the distance. On the way, driving up north Eye stopped by to see my grandparents first. My grandmother said, "If Eye were you Eye'd wait it all out until his trial. Eye'm not going to tell you not to go because you're grown but you're doing so well for yourself and Eye don't want you to end up in trouble." My grandmother was extremely wise and Eye should've listened to her but the love Eye had for my family in spite of the differences kept me focused on leaving.

Rick and Eye make it up north and instead of going directly to my parent's house; we go straight to Kurt's home where Jerome would be waiting on Rick. Eye called my mother to let her know that we were in town. Eye decided to go through Kurt's mail to see if there were any past due bills so Eye could pay them before they lapsed. Eye began doing a little cleaning just to get my mind off of things. Eye drove to my parent's house to see if they were going to go visit Kurt but it wasn't a visiting day so the only people that could visit him was an attorney or member of clergy. Well, Eye was a licensed minister so Eye was able to visit Kurt. Eye knew what cops did to innocent people so it was up to me to make sure my brother was okay. Kurt told me that one of the detectives punched him in the face, but he didn't want to get all into that. Eye wanted to know what happened but Eye allowed his attorney to get all of that information. When Eye drove back to my parents Eye let them know that he was okay. Eye didn't bother to tell them a detective punched him in the face because Eye didn't want to add to them already worrying. Once again Eye became my brother's keeper, only this time it was my eldest brother. This was very puzzling to me because Kurt was a comedian, not a murderer. This was a defining moment because it showed Kurt who his true friends were and those that were only attached to him because of what he possessed or the things he had access to.

There are some people who YOU'VE ACCEPTED as a "Friend" that:

(1) Only became your friend to devour your character because they're jealous/ envious of your drawing power

(2) Are delusional into believing you want more than a friendship

(3) Are awaiting the correct moment to try and destroy what you're building

(4) Have become your friend because they THOUGHT you were part of a certain group, wanted to TRY you, but realized you were a horse from a different stable

(5) Are trying to become more than; to gain your TRUST, only to betray you

(6) You've known prior to social media and they still have feelings for you and will also deny you, etc.

There are also people YOU'VE DENIED that:

(1) Would've had your best interest at heart
(2) Is capable of being a true friend
(3) Would be a warrior on your behalf
(4) Could enhance your life/ lifestyle, etc.

POINT: Your life's experiences differ from that of the person YOU'RE CONNECTING with. YOUR interpretation, perception, or value may also differ! Time to evaluate and make the necessary cuts!! Kingdom/ Empire Building BEGIN with YOU!! - Lamont Bershawn.

    The next morning, my mother called and asked if Eye wanted to go to church with her, Eye really wasn't in the mood to go anywhere so Eye declined. Eye needed to get some air so Eye went to grab a few items from the supermarket. When Eye arrived back at the house one of Kurt's friends was there to see if it was anything they could do. Eye thought the gesture was nice because she was the first person outside of family that seemed to care. Jerome received a call later that day from the cousin of one of Kurt's "live in" friends. A "live in" friend as Eye considered it to be was actually a freeloader. The moment Kurt was arrested, the "live in" began stealing some of Kurt's valuables {jewelry, fur coats, money, etc.}. The cousin of the "live in" alerted Jerome that some of Kurt's valuables were over her house. Jerome was adamant on retrieving Kurt's property, so he was looking forward to Troy {the live in} to show up. The phone constantly rang, but Eye allowed the answering machine to answer a few calls, anyone really important had my cell phone number. This one particular time the phone rang Eye decided to answer and it was Troy. Troy was very shocked to hear my voice and he asked, "What my plans were the rest of the day?" Eye told him who was at the house and we were planning on either going bowling or catching a movie. He wanted to know if he could join us and if Eye could pick him up. Rick, Jerome and Eye went to pick him up because we had to make a few more stops before going back to the house. We stopped by the mall to get an air mattress and then by the gas station. Eye thought everything was okay because we greeted each other with a handshake and everyone seemed to be in better spirits.

When we get in the house awaiting the ladies to return before we headed bowling Jerome punches Troy in the mouth. Jerome stands over Troy and asks him, "Where the fuck is my brother's belongings? Eye'm sure you have them because your cousin called me and told me." Jerome then pulls out a set of handcuffs and placed Troy's hands behind him and handcuffed him. He stood Troy up and walked him downstairs. Rick and Eye stood there in amazement looking at each other. When Jerome came back upstairs Eye asked him, "what the hell was all that about?" Jerome responded, "Eye want answers. Kurt opens his house to these people and they take advantage of him." Eye knew Jerome was hot headed and wasn't a logical thinker. It was at that moment Eye knew the devil himself was staging the atmosphere and it wasn't great. Too much was going on and my stomach started hurting, so Eye had to use the restroom. Rick was outside smoking a cigarette and Jerome was downstairs. The doorbell rang and Eye heard a woman's voice, Eye thought it was the people we were waiting on but it was Jerome's current girlfriend, Cecilia. Eye cracked the door open and all Eye could hear was Cecilia on her cell phone speaking with her girlfriend saying, "Troy is here, Jerome have him downstairs." In an instant Eye yelled for Jerome to come here. Eye was clean and out the bathroom by the time Jerome came upstairs. Eye pulled him in the room where Cecilia couldn't hear me.

Eye told Jerome to get downstairs and get Troy out of this house now. He responded shaking his head profusely saying, "Okay." Jerome went and walked his girlfriend outside while he gave her the keys to his car to drive. When Eye went downstairs Eye find that Troy is still there. Now the kicker was Jerome's girlfriend was Troy's ex-girlfriend. Damn! Can't he deal with someone that no one close to him dealt with?

Nevertheless, something spoke to me within my spirit and told me plainly to leave because this isn't the atmosphere you created. Eye disregarded the voice that spoke within my spirit. Eye went to the basement and saw that Troy was tied to a fucking chair and his braids were cut. The only thing that was hurt was his feelings. At that moment Jerome was trying to get a confession. Eye left from downstairs and Jerome and Rick followed behind me. The problem with that was Jerome still never untied Troy and he unknowingly left his cell phone beside him. When we got to the living room Eye blasted Jerome for doing dumb shit, yet Eye never left the house. Approximately five minutes later a rapid, hard and repetitive knock hit the door. Just by the sound Eye knew it was trouble for us. Jerome jumped off the couch and was about to run downstairs. Eye told him to sit his ass down. Eye proceeded to open the door. It was four police officers. Eye asked them, "What's going on officer?" An officer replied, "We received a call that someone was being held against their will. Who's in the house? Eye told him exactly who was in the house from the top floor to the basement. Eye asked him if he had the correct address. He called out an address but it was the incorrect address, which gave me a second of a relief, then he gave the correct address.

One officer went upstairs, one went in the basement and two were in the living room placing us in handcuffs. Jerome identified himself as a school police officer to the Sergeant. When the Sergeant came upstairs, he looked at Jerome and said, "Eye'm surprised at you." Here we are headed to the precinct to get booked on some charges. Once again, denying my spirit Eye was in trouble over some shit Jerome did. Eye started thinking, "Eye should have let his ass continue downstairs and he'd have to answer to the charges alone." We get to the police precinct and our attorney gets called to meet us there. We were being charged with simple assault. While we're speaking with our attorney The County detectives come in and extradite us {Rick, Jerome and myself} to the County. Eye knew this wasn't good and some bullshit had taken place because this was the same place my oldest brother, Kurt was being held.

The next morning, we go before the judge for arraignment and it's the same bitch that Eye was in front of a few years back when Jerome lied on me. When she read the charges, there were ten more charges added to the simple assault. She gave us a bail of $500,000.00 cash, with the most serious of the charges being kidnapping. The prosecutors tried their best to link both cases together but they couldn't because their case was getting weaker by the moment. Here Eye'm thinking, "What the fuck did Eye get into. My grandmother pretty much begged me not to come up here." To make a long story short, we stayed in the county jail for ninety-three days because our bail was lowered by the President Judge to $100,000.00 cash. This was the most nervous Eye'd ever been in my life because Eye really didn't know what to expect. Eye looked back at my dad and he nodded which made me feel a little comfortable. When we left the court a few of the correctional officers said, "They're trying to railroad you guys, and if Eye were you Eye'd sue the pants off this county." Well, that wasn't on my mind at the present moment, the only thing Eye could think of was getting the hell out of here. Do Eye take responsibility for my actions? Absolutely! Eye should have followed my mind or listened to the "VOICE."

Let's see if we've ever REALLY recognized the "VOICE!"

The "Voice" has many names {intuition, instinct, consciousness/ conscience, "God" within, Chi, inner man, power that be, etc.}.

(1) Have you ever been somewhere and the "Voice" spoke with you telling you to "Get the hell out of this place NOW?" {You listened only to find out something bad happened moments after your departure!!}

(2) Have you ever been driving and the "Voice" took you on another route, contrary to your normal way of travel? {Later to find out you avoided a fatal accident!!}

(3) Have you ever ignored the "Voice" and found yourself in trouble? {Happens daily with people}

(4) Have you missed out on a "Blessing" by following someone else's path instead of listening to the "Voice?" {Of course}

(5) Have you and your friend ever been at a location and the "Voice" told you to "Immediately leave these premises?"

Your friend looked at your expression and dropped everything to follow you!!

{Your friend tells you Eye saw a look in your eye that ALERTED me. That was the power of discernment within your friend to recognize the power within you. Later to find out, the location you left got robbed and someone was murdered.}.

{The above are examples of coincidences that may have been a similarity in your life}

The "VOICE" is YOUR PERSONAL "SPIRITUAL GOD/ FORCE" that directs/ guides YOU!! The reason NOBODY else can hear the "Voice" that YOU hear is because it's designed distinctively for YOU. It's there to protect and guide you so RECOGNIZE IT, RESPECT IT and REACT/ RESPOND TO IT!!

The Liar That Lingers in the Closet

    We took a plea for simple assault and had everything else dismissed under our lawyer's recommendation. Eye knew this would be my very last straw of allowing someone to get me caught up in some mess.

    Allow me to address the issue concerning Jerome's involvement with the School Police. Jerome never took the test to become a school police officer. He was really close with one of our former teacher's that worked as a Professor but was also a real police officer for the housing developments. He refused to get Jerome involved in the housing development police so he pulled a few strings to get Jerome a school police job. Jerome loved to be in authoritative positions and it went to his head. He really thought that (1) he was above the law and (2) he was a sworn officer of the law. Jerome worked that gig part-time and only while school was in. Jerome ended up getting fired from the school police because he was fighting students. It was probably best because he worked in a middle school and was making sexual advances to those young ladies. Jerome's girlfriend thought he was an officer of the law because he carried a gun and had a badge. School police officers don't carry firearms.

    One weekend Jerome and his girlfriend were driving to North Carolina and he was pulled over for speeding in Maryland. When the officer asked for Jerome's identification instead of him giving the officer his driver's license Jerome presented his school police officer's badge. Two things wrong with this situation (1) he was just fired from his job and should have turned in his badge and the rest of his credentials {he was impersonating an officer} and (2) he had a loaded firearm in his vehicle. He ended up going to jail, losing his girlfriend and getting his gun taken from him. My mother bailed him out of jail and hired a great attorney that had a lot of pull, but he wasn't cheap. He ended up getting Jerome off, but he wasn't able to get his gun back and his now ex- girlfriend knew that he was famous for telling lies. Jerome seemed to stay in trouble and the best thing about all of it was Eye was nowhere around him.

"*Learn to accept people for who they are and stop trying to accept them for the potential that you see within them. Some people will*

never achieve the potential or credit you're giving them because of the lack of internal wisdom, low self-esteem, or living in past hurts." - Lamont Bershawn.

His friends began comparing him to me in more ways than one because they were truly beginning to see him for the person he really was. Once again, Jerome started hating me for the things his friends were telling him while making the comparisons. This was the defining moment that Jerome would cut me out of all of our pictures because he no longer wanted people to know that he had a twin brother.

My mother refused to give up on him although he cost her lots of money. My dad wasn't getting involved in paying anymore legal fees for people that did stupid shit. Even after high school Jerome wanted to join the Army. Now that Eye think of it Eye'm guessing he saw himself as a complete fuck up and felt the need to get rehabilitated through military. Jerome went a signed up and Eye was happy for him, especially if that was going to give him a better sense of respect for himself. Eye'd never thought of joining the Army but my mother didn't want him to go in alone. Mom looked at me and said, "Please don't let him go in the military all alone because he's going to need a friend and Eye know you won't allow anything to happen to him." Eye told her, "He won't be alone because they'll be other people there for him to meet." My mother began to cry, so Eye signed to go in together on the "buddy team." Eye knew military wasn't for me but Eye did join to make my mother happy. Once again, "Eye'm acting as my brother's keeper."

A few months in my moral begin to get low and Eye no longer have the desire to be there. Eye walk up to the platoon Sergeant and tell him, "Eye don't even feel like being here any longer." Let me be honest and say, "Jerome and Eye knew about camping because my parents taught us how to survive the outdoors. My mother took us camping and my dad got us involved in hunting at the age of twelve." We were infantry soldiers and they loved the outdoors no matter the temperature and we'd bivouac {camp without cover} for days. Hell, we were on the "buddy system", so Eye became smart and began thinking like a soldier should. In other words, when they had something hard designed for us Eye made it a little easier. Most drill sergeants were happy and pleased because we showed them some of our survival techniques. Jerome took that to a whole new level. Eye was pretty much the quiet brother, but very observant. Jerome was the one that told people believable stories that became very interesting. One evening the military had movie night for the troops. The movie was "Total Recall" with Arnold Schwarzenegger.

The conversation between Jerome and the First Sergeant seemed to be one that the sergeant thought would inspire the entire platoon, so instead of watching the movie Jerome and Eye became the center of attention. The sergeant gave a brief introduction about the lives he thought we had and we took center stage. Jerome was a professional liar, so he did all of the talking.

The lights all of a sudden turned on and one of the Drill Sergeants stood on the stage and said, "We're proud to have a couple of celebrities in our midst. We decided to stop the movie in order to allow these individuals to take the stage and tell us about their lives as celebrities and why they decided to join the United States Army. As I present these young men, I want you to stand to your feet and give them a standing ovation."

When Jerome and I walked on the stage, after the clapping there was total silence as if they couldn't wait to hear what we had to say. Jerome did a majority of the talking because he's the one that wanted the attention. I was up there to make sure he didn't stumble on his lie since I heard it before. Jerome told them where we were from and named a list of movies that his Sifu was in that I had very little knowledge of. First question from the audience, "What kind of car do you drive?" Jerome responded, "Midnight blue 300SD Mercedes" and my brother have a "Pearl black 300SD." I'm thinking to myself, "That's what our father drives." Second question, "You said that you choreographed the Last Dragon. Can you give us a martial arts demonstration?"

Well, that was the easy part because we both knew Kung Fu. Jerome and I performed the "Long arm attacker and defender form."

We received another standing ovation and word got around the entire military base. Needless to say, we were liked and hated but still got along with the majority. The next day we're taught hand to hand combat and all eyes are on us. I have to say that Jerome played his role. When he was up to fight with the baton, he did a forward roll and stood up hitting his opponent knocking him down. The instructors were impressed because they never saw anyone enter the ring that way. When my turn came to fight with the baton, they were expecting something spectacular, but instead I remained focus and used the baton to kick up his left leg and the other end of the baton to hit in his chest. Yep, it was a scene from the movie, "Coming to America." We were on a roll putting a few real techniques into action. We were into martial arts and camping out so those things came easy.

Later that evening we were told to take our poncho and tie it to a tree and make half of a tent in the event it rain. Everyone tied their poncho to a tree, but Jerome and I used the same tree which made a full tent, but no one else picked up on it. One of the Drill Sergeants came over the next morning, and said, "You guys were the only ones that used common sense and tied your ponchos to the same tree. Brilliant!" Another Drill Sergeant walked by a said, "I hope you guys don't think that you're special." The Company Commander smiled and said, "You're just mad those gentlemen aren't in your platoon. Keep up the great work gentlemen." We responded, "Yes Sir!"

We blended in well with everyone although my thought was, "Why in the hell did I sign my life away for a military that don't give a damn about me? It hit me at that point harder than it ever did, "I made a life sacrifice because I'd do anything to keep a smile on my mother's face." One of the drill sergeants enjoyed making different cadences {songs to march to} that most of us could relate to just to make the march or run a little easier. My favorite was the cadence about the Flintstones cartoon:

"Pebbles and Bam-Bam on a Friday night

Trying to get to heaven on a paper kite

Lightning struck (BOOM) and down they fell (AHHH)

Instead of getting to heaven, they went straight to hell

Dino the dog (RUFF RUFF) was on the bone (CHOMP CHOMP)

While Fred and Barney rocked the microphone

There was nothing that Fred or Barney could do

'cept sing "Yabba daba daba daba daaaaaba do!"

    One afternoon after drills a few of the guys went to the Exchange Center for free time to do a little shopping before Christmas break. I didn't feel up to going so I stayed inside the dorm to write a few letters. One of the drill instructors came in and saw me sitting on the bed writing. When he walked over towards me, I stood up and stood in the parade rest position. He said, "At ease soldier." He began talking to me about my plans for Christmas Exodus and my goals with the military. I told him, "The only reason I joined was because my mother didn't want my brother to join the military by himself. When she started crying it hurt my heart and I joined just to satisfy her." The drill sergeant said, "You're not required to stay if you really don't want to be here." I asked him, "How can I get out of this contract with the Army? I don't want to disappoint anyone." He responded, "The only person you'll be disappointing is yourself by living out someone else's dream for your life instead of your very own." I began thinking about the things I really desired doing and getting my life back.
    When the fellas returned from the Exchange center it was time for everyone to order the insignia for the uniforms to go to the barber to get our hair cut. When we returned to the dorm a couple of the guys

felt the need to clean up behind the barber with using a straight razor for a cleaner and smoother look. All that decided to join in and get a smoother look almost got in trouble but it was overlooked. Me and Jerome's uniform came back with the "wrong" patch, but it was too late to return for the correct one. The moment arrived and we were in route to catch the flight back home. When we arrived at the airport home Jerome pulled out two red berets for us to put on our heads. I asked Jerome, "What's this for?" He said, "It matches the patch on our uniform." When we got off the airplane my parents along with Tanisha and Darla were waiting for us. We hugged everyone, grabbed our bag and headed to the house. When we arrived at the house we settled in and immediately gathered in the living room and began talking.

Darla and I were previously involved years prior but we remained friends, the same with Jerome and Tanisha. Darla was the second person to write me a letter while I was in the Army. My mother was the first of course letting me know how proud she was of the both of us. Darla would always encourage me and she'd always send updated photos of herself. Being in the infantry unit, we hardly saw any women unless we went to sick call or saw the supply specialist in the field.

My father asked, "How long is your break?" I replied, "Two weeks." My father replied, "Great. We can have a little father and son time together." "Absolutely", I responded. My mother was happy to see that Darla and I kept in touch. Mom always saw Darla as being her daughter in law. I guess it was because my mother saw so much of herself in Darla as a child being mistreated by her mother. Darla and I were childhood sweethearts and we always were in church together singing. During the two-week vacation I enjoyed myself with my family, but knew that I had to leave once again. I guess it wouldn't have been so bad if my family wasn't so close.

There was so much going on in Darla's home, that she was actually tired of being there and dealing with her own mother to the point that she considered my mother her very own. Prior to me leaving for the military I gave Darla her space to deal with her issues, while I began my psychological preparation for the change that was about to take place in my life. My mother asked me to go see Darla before I left for the military. The day before I left, I called Darla to see if she was free to talk in person. I went to see Darla that afternoon and when I got down there, she was sitting on her step with her head down. I walked over to her and when she looked up, she had tears in her eyes and said, "I'm sorry, I didn't ever want our friendship to come to an end. You're my best friend and now you're leaving me." I responded, "Darla, you'll always be special and one day you're going to find that person that will be perfect for you. You know the only reason I'm going is to please my mother." Darla responded, "When are you going to live for yourself instead of always pleasing someone else's desires?" I told Darla, "This is where we're similar. We both desire to please our mothers, but you've become tired of playing the mother role. I'm a man and I just don't like my mother being out there being underappreciated. The least I could do to make her happy is join the military. How would I deal with the thought of her worrying about Jerome being alone with nobody to depend on? She's already dealing with the worries of having a brain tumor.

When we returned back to the military base after Exodus the sergeant asked me, "Do you still want out?" Eye responded, "Absolutely." It was a few more weeks before graduation and my sergeant got word to the Colonel. On graduation day, Eye went before the Colonel. The Colonel said, "It's not my intention to keep a man in the military against their God given will." The sergeant said, "Eye don't understand why recruiters tell people lies in order to make a quota."

"Soldier, it is hereby ordered on this date that you are released from all duties as an active duty soldier in the United States Army. Thanks for your dedication Lamont, good luck on your journey." {Colonel signed}.

Six months later, Eye received my Honorable Discharge from the United States Army. Jerome began telling people that the only reason Eye was released was because Eye was suicidal, but what do you expect from someone that enjoy telling lies?

Jerome was involved with Tammy who was an awesome hairstylist and I was involved with Darla who lived a few doors away from Tammy. Darla's mother Miss Penny was actually the pianist. A few times Jerome and I went over to Miss Penny house to visit the young ladies whether it was for a birthday party, choir rehearsal or one of their family gatherings. One evening Jerome and I was leaving Miss Penny house and Jerome saw Tammy outside and he approached Tammy. I clearly heard Tammy ask him, "Aren't you involved with Tanisha?" Jerome replied, "No, we're friends. My brother is dating Darla."

The next thing I realize Jerome is hanging over Tammy's house. It actually caused a problem between Tammy and Tanisha because of Jerome's lie. Things became hectic at times but it simmered down when Tammy became pregnant. Darla and Tanisha were both beautiful, but Tanisha was a boxer. The day Tammy gave birth to her baby, Darla and Tanisha were the first ones to arrive. Jerome and I heard the news and we immediately went to the hospital to see the newborn baby, Jerome's first born.

When we arrived at the hospital, we see my Aunt Betty, who is actually Tammy's nurse. When I saw the pretty little girl, I knew she belonged to Jerome just by looking at her nose. I called my grandmother and said, "She's a winner." They named her, Mercedes after the car. Tammy wanted to straighten up her life and move out of the ghetto so she stopped doing hair and went back to school to become a nurse. Tammy couldn't trust Jerome to take care of Mercedes because he loved running the streets too much so she asked my mother if she could handle the responsibility. My mother welcomed the idea especially if Tammy wanted to better her lifestyle.

Everyone knew Jerome was like a leaf in the wind and only cared about himself. He ended up going to Maryland for the weekend and called me while he was there knowing that I was at a church convention. We met up and he introduced me to Gabby. Gabby was a very nice person that was very much into the church but she ended up falling in love with Jerome after he impregnated her. Gabby ended up having the baby but Jerome never acknowledged his son although the DNA test was ninety-nine percent positive.

Jerome did everything to try and cover up his homosexual lifestyle. He loved hanging around known homosexuals in order to bully or take advantage of them. One weekend a couple of our female friends came to visit us. Our cousin Peter and his lover was visiting as well and we went to New York because they never been and also because they wanted to go shopping the next day.

Later that evening after we checked into the hotel room in New York the ladies wanted to ride around to see the nightlife. Peter wanted us to drop him off at the "all men night club" and Jerome wanted to tag along with Peter. Peter looked at me and said, "I knew Jerome was part of the churn." I asked Peter, "What is the churn?" Peter replied, "The churn is another name for the homosexual lifestyle." I was totally shocked that Jerome would rather go to the club with Peter opposed to show the women around New York's nightlife. I began reminiscing and calculating different situations when Jerome was comfortable wearing string bikini underwear, trying on my mother's shoes, kissing a man's penis, watching gay porn, when his ex-girlfriend caught him looking at naked men while masturbating and wearing women's jeans to name a few.

Jerome hates me for several reasons beyond my control. I'm a Published Author, an ordained Elder/ Bishop, I'm out here doing webinars, interviews, podcasts and I only involve myself with one woman at a time. We have two totally different lifestyles.

Jerome feels comfortable and complete by pulling people in with his lies while I encourage people with the truth. Most of the women that he's dealt with tell him that I'm the better-looking twin and last but not least he's afraid to come outside of the closet and be his authentic self while I'm enjoying living my truth. It's sad but very true that the only use Jerome has for a woman is to use her and abuse her. If she's not in a position to take care of him, she's worthless. Jerome gets a majority of his suits handed down to him by homosexuals although I know he's told so many people that his tailor made the suit for him.

Once again Eye was free from feeling obligated to allow people to see the liar Jerome was and it wouldn't have any bearing on me because we looked alike. It became tiring and Eye was getting exhausted of him thinking that Eye followed him places but more exhausted of people considering us the same because we looked alike.

"When you look in the mirror, what are you seeing? "IF" you don't like what you're looking at, you have the power to change it. Once you begin to really appreciate your exterior, your interior will begin to change. Your reflection speaks volumes!! The greatest story ever told is NOT that of Jesus, but it's the one that's being written as you're living your OWN life!!"
----> THE LIVING WORD <--- Lamont Bershawn.

SHEDDING SOME LIGHT!!

Eye constantly hear people accuse myself and others of spreading "False" doctrine. Allow me to explain to some of you indoctrinated ass people EXACTLY what this means, since you'd rather sit in church and refuse to STUDY TO SHOW YOURSELVES APPROVED UNTO YOUR GOD!!

Let's define doctrine. According to the online dictionary doctrine is defined as a particular principle, position, or policy taught or advocated, as of a religion or government.

Do you see the words "Taught" and "Advocated" {to speak or write in favor of; support or urge by argument; recommend publicly}. In other words, whatever rules, laws, regulations, dogma, principle, discipline that your church, organization, belief system that's a part thereof; ANYTHING going AGAINST or is NOT mentioned in the system YOU "Be- LIE-Ve" will be considered FALSE.

Does it mean that because it's NOT in the religious beliefs that YOU follow, that it's "False" doctrine? ABSOLUTELY NOT!!

It just means (1) you have not learned of it as of yet (2) You are a closed minded individual {not willing to learn more information, but comfortable "knowing" what you have in your mind} (3) have a LIMITED perception (4) Have made the system you're a part of a "God" and therefore have enslaved yourself by conforming to a religious practice that have NOTHING to do with God/ Creator

(5) You've spoken/ judged someone out of PURE IGNORANCE, etc.

When following religious doctrine according to the groups: 33% {Christians}, 21% {Muslims}, 13% {Hindu}, 6% {Buddhist}, 15% {Atheist} and 11% are {TOTALLY CONFUSED ABOUT ALL OF IT}!!

Why does Christianity hold more weight than any other religion? It's because Christianity is a manmade religion that's a conglomeration {to form or gather into a mass or whole} of ALL religion combined.

Whatever religion YOU follow or book YOU abide by someone in there said, "LEARN." It would be wise to "LEARN" prior to making judgments against someone that refuse to follow the curriculum that you choose to follow or live according to. "In all the information you're receiving, remember to receive an understanding!!"

When my first book, "Bishops Need Love Too" was released Eye received 4.75 stars out of 5 with twenty-five reviews. Eye released the book under a pseudonym under the advice of my publisher to protect everyone's identity including my own. It was one of my greatest accomplishments achieved but Jerome became jealous, irate and envious. He decided to write a review to attack my character but Eye wasn't bothered because it was expected. Eye began seeing women that were rejected by me because they had psychological issues, women that still carried grudges because they didn't go to my prom with me, women Jerome tried to hook me up with but weren't my type and women that disliked me because my religious views differed from theirs on Jerome's team. Eye realized that these women weren't really upset with me; they just wanted my attention and thought by getting closer to Jerome they'd receive it. Eye knew they really had no interest in dating him because they knew he had a passion for looking at naked men, at least that's what one of his ex- girlfriends said. Eye asked her was that the reason she decided to break things off, but she never responded. Jerome was an opportunist among other things. It didn't matter what the situation might be or consisted of, even if he had to deny his friends. Jerome had a friend that loved to sing and he called Jerome to let him know that God told him to tell Jerome that he could no longer be his friend. What this friend didn't know was that Jerome put in a bid to use him to get next to the millionaire he introduced Jerome to. It meant that Jerome had to plant negative seeds in the millionaire head and slander his name. Jerome asked me to talk to his friend because he was hurt that he no longer wanted anything to do with him. Eye told Jerome he needed to understand what loyalty means. Jerome would've never been introduced to the millionaire if it weren't for his friend.

"As you browse through your "Friends" list trying to figure out their nature, intention or motive; understand that they may not be an enemy, but an opportunist.

An opportunist is an individual that sits dormant awaiting the chance to use you as leverage for the purpose of gain or will wait for the opportune time to crumble your foundation. Their intention or goal has risen beyond infatuation. It's more of a "Fatal Attraction" or an "Obsession."

These individuals have been lurking in the shadows watching and critiquing your every move. You've become their study, their project, their "ace in the hole." You've been plagiarized and your patent has been copied, but you have yet to receive your royalties or credit for your creativity."

POINT: *We connect to people all of the time. A connection can be for the purpose of networking/ business, spiritual reasons,* *sexual desires {let's be real...lol}, religious affiliations, etc. When opportunity knocks, is it always beneficial for you or could you be opening the door to your demise? - Lamont Bershawn.*

Most people would probably be asking, "Why did Eye continue being a true brother to Jerome even though he had no good intentions towards me?" Eye'd try my best to please my mother because Eye knew what Eye saw her go through. The last thing she needed was to see her children at odds with each other. Eye'd give Jerome chance after chance to get his life in order, but each time it failed.

The upsetting thing about it all is that every year it seems to be repetitive. Last year we stopped speaking for five months. He flew out to Atlanta to support the event. We shook hands and hugged one another, afterwards we told each other that we loved each other. That was a priceless moment.

I heard someone say, "look at what prayer can do." I kindly responded, "This wasn't prayer. We just decided to place our differences aside and respect each other."

Life's too short for the bullshit. Especially, to allow other people's mess to infiltrate family or a brotherhood.

The "Cracked Mirror" or the shattered glass became even clearer as I began to pay more attention to Jerome.

1. Jerome lied about earning any of the degrees he presents.
2. Jerome lied about being a police officer.
3. Jerome lied about being a detective.
4. Jerome lied about pedophilia tendencies.
5. Jerome lied about cutting Dave brake line.
6. Jerome lied about stealing $10,000.00 from Doc.
7. Jerome lied about living in a 10,000 square feet home.
8. Jerome lied about having sex with my previous female involvements.
9. Jerome lied about his infatuation with naked or gay men.
10. Jerome lied about kissing a man dick.

11. Jerome lied about stealing from me.
12. Jerome lied about filing me on his taxes as his mentally ill brother.
13. Jerome lied about his occupation.
14. Jerome is a convicted felon.
15. Jerome isn't an ordained member of clergy.
16. Jerome isn't a licensed chiropractor.
17. Jerome is a habitual liar and thief.
18. Jerome is a narcissist.
19. Jerome made a statement to detective to help keep brother incarcerated.
20. Jerome slept with his incarcerated brother wife.
21. Jerome has two children but only claims one.
22. Jerome is a womanizer.
23. Jerome lied about being an accomplished actor.
24. Jerome is a great embellisher.
25. Jerome is a sadist.
26. Jerome threatened to kill me.
27. Jerome lied on me in order for me to have a tarnished record like him.
28. Jerome tried to get me killed by police by lying on me.
29. Jerome tells everyone's personal business.
30. Jerome is a very deadly and dangerous individual.
31. Jerome never bodyguarded for the Gambino Crime Family.
32. Jerome never saved a girl from drowning in the Atlantic Ocean.
33. Jerome is an opportunist.
34. Jerome lied about me being suicidal.
35. Jerome lied about being Frank Lucas caretaker for three year.

Jerome lied about everything that make him feel obsolete or that he can't fit into a slot above everyone else. When Jerome looks at you as a potential threat or his competition, he becomes nervous that other people begin praising you and he becomes obsolete. It's imperative that Jerome must be the center of attention at all times. Jerome have mentioned to me on several occasions that he could kill me and get away with it. This is why Jerome must destroy your character and get everyone thinking negatively about you using lie after lie. Jerome did a radio interview and lied throughout the interview to gain attention or followers. He claimed the Gambino crime family hired him as their personal bodyguard. How could that be when Jerome volunteered as a Guardian Angel? The founder, Curtis Sliwa spoke against the Gambino crime family on radio which would be a conflict of interest.

Please take note and understand that there are people who are upset with you because you made a conscious decision to dismember and disconnect from them.

They're bitter because they thought plagiarizing you would benefit them in their lives. They discredited, devalued, disrespected and tried their best to dismantle you at every level.

They had no idea the only reason people sought them out was because of their connection or attachment to you.

Those same people are trying their best to get your attention by keeping your name in their mouth.

Don't become sidetracked, lose focus or feel the desire to retaliate to the negativity. Every time they look into the mirror, they see the reflection of you!! Why? It's because they're used to living behind the mask of someone else!!

S/N: Be watchful of that individual that will not only tell a lie but feels comfortable investing in their lie in order to bring you into their lie that you "be-LIE-ve!!"

Eye can only be M.E. (Metaphysically Evolving)!! – Lamont Bershawn.

Jerome is poisonous and full of venom. Be careful because he'll strike when you least expect it!!

You have to be careful of the information "You" entertain; because with it comes the spirit that endorse it.

IF you're NOT strong enough to handle the spirit that endorse it. You can end up being confused trying to find "Righteousness" in an atmosphere of "Unrighteousness" and You CAN'T find TRUTH when the FOUNDATION of it is a LIE!!!

Learn to keep contrary, conflicting, compromising and cunning folk out of your presence. They only "cloud" your perception and positive atmosphere. - Lamont Bershawn

Misery Poem

Hey bro! Listen to me,
Everyone knows that you live a life full of misery,
Living a life full of lies 'til no end,
So much shit, where do I begin?

Shall I start with your abundant acting career,
Or impersonating an officer year after year?
Your entire life is like that of the tooth fairy,
Just like that dude that sucked your dick that sang like a "Canary."

I asked you to go your separate way,
Instead you want to come for me day by day,
Making up lies to get folk on your side,
Start telling the truth and put aside your pride.

You're a convicted felon and labeled liar,
You know the song, "Liar, liar pants on fire."
A ten thousand square feet home, where?
Misery will forever keep you living in fear.

Continue hiding behind the old Rolls,
While pimpin' the old punks and lonely hoes.
Tell the truth and begin living free,
Oops I forgot that house belongs to our mommy.

Those fake gold records hanging on the wall,
Yep they're a conversation piece that's all,
Your own friends have investigated you,
Laughing behind your back Knowing that your words aren't true.

Lamont Bershawn

You're a wanna be my brother,
Stop acting like a fucking sucker.
I will admit that you're determined as can be,
Just a reminder, you'll get nowhere living in misery.

- Lamont Bershawn. {Original Piece}.

Misery

This is a part of my life that I'll never forget as long as I live. People say, "Everything happens for a reason, in its time and due season." Well, all I have to say is, "I've learned a valuable lesson."

In December 2002, I was living in Florida, working at Cendant Mortgage in the morning and the Pepsi Company in the evenings.

It was early Wednesday morning; I had just arrived at Cendant Mortgage when I received a phone call from Jerome. It wasn't unusual for him to call; we talked at least every other day. When I answered the phone, he paused and asked me if I was sitting down. I said, "I just arrived at work, what's up?" He said, "Have you heard?" "Heard what?" I replied. "Is mom okay?" He said, "Yes, but our Kurt was being framed for murder."

I immediately logged onto the computer to see if this was real. My first thought was I being "Punk'd." To my shocking eyes, there was a photo of Kurt handcuffed and being taken out of the courthouse to jail. My day was spoiled, and I really couldn't think clear. My Supervisor came over to me and asked, "Are you alright? You look as if you just lost your best friend." I showed my Supervisor the story on the internet. She said, "Go ahead, and take the day off." I left the job and went straight to my grandparent's home to make sure they were okay. They were just as shocked as I was.

I called my supervisor and told her that I'm going to need to take emergency leave. My leave was granted. I called my boss at the Pepsi Company and told him what happened and that I'm going to need to take emergency leave. That too was granted. It really didn't matter if it was granted or not, I knew in my spirit that I needed to be in Pennsylvania to support my family. I called Jerome up, he said, "When you come you may as well bring Pete up. He can help you drive to avoid that long train ride." I knew my brother talked about allowing Pete to come up to live with him in order to get a new surrounding and pretty much start a new life. I called Pete and told him the news. He said, "I'll be ready to leave whenever you say the word." That's what I liked about Pete; he wasn't the type of person to hold anyone up. He was prompt.

On Friday afternoon, December 20, 2002 we were on the road headed to Pennsylvania. We knew it would be a twelve-hour trip so while one drove the other slept. When we arrived in Pennsylvania early that Saturday morning, we stopped by my parent's house.

We were eager to get to Kurt's home. We went over there because we knew with the recent situation; there were probably a few bills that needed to be taken care of. My parents picked me up and we went to visit him in jail, but it wasn't a visiting day, but because I was clergy, he was entitled to a clerical visit. I just wanted to make sure he was okay. He was very happy to see that I made it in town to see him. I told him that mom and dad were outside, but they weren't able to see him because it wasn't his visiting day. I didn't ask him what happened, because deep down on the inside I knew he wasn't a murderer. He wanted to explain things to me, but I told him to explain it to his attorney. I went outside after visiting with him for about fifteen minutes and let my parents know that he was in good spirits.

We left the jail and I went back to my brother's home to get things together, vacuum. I began listening to music. When I arrived at my brother's home; Pete, and a couple of Kurt's' friends were there making sure everything was okay. Nothing much happened that evening, except we ordered pizza, and watched movies to keep our minds occupied.

Early Sunday morning around 9:00 a.m., my mother called me to see if I wanted to go to church with her. I said, "No." I normally would've gone, but I really wasn't in the mood. I woke up and started rearranging things in the house.

You know, I just couldn't get my mind off "My brother, the comedian was being charged with murder." It just didn't add up.

My father hired this Muslim attorney, who was often compared to attorney Johnnie Cochran. Well, that was like riding in a Chrysler 300 telling people it was a Bentley. In other words, it wasn't the same. Nevertheless, it was the attorney that a cousin recommended, who at that time worked for the District Attorney's office. We had never been in this type of situation, or to this magnitude so we didn't know who to get as a lawyer.

Later that Sunday afternoon, we decided we'd go bowling, but first we had to make a stop at the mall. The phone rang before we left the house; it was Craig, the young man my brother took in under his wing, because he had nowhere else to go. I answered the phone. Craig said, "Is this Lamont?" I said, "It is." Craig responded, "Hello sir, when did you arrive in town?" I said, "Saturday morning." I told him that we were going bowling in a few hours, but we were going to go by the mall first. He said, "Do you mind if I come along with you guys. I'd like to go, but I don't have any money." I said, "It's cool, I can give you fifty dollars."

He said, "I'm getting ready now, as a matter of fact, I'm right down the street from the mall can you swing by and get me?" So, Pete and I went to pick Craig up. We dropped Jerome off at the mall so he could pick up the air mattress that he wanted to buy. We went by the mall, walked around for an hour and then we returned back to the house.

When we arrived in the house Paula and Tina are on the couch drinking juice awaiting our arrival. Out of nowhere Jerome punches Craig in the mouth and handcuffed him, then proceed on taking him to the basement. I could tell by Pete's expression that he too was shocked at the current event. At that moment Paula and Tina decided to leave the house and my spirit was telling me to leave too, but the other half of my brain went into protective mode. It was as if God was giving me a choice, either stay and face the consequences or leave and you'll hear about the death of your loved one.

Craig use to live there, so they went downstairs. I wondered what was going on in the basement so I went to check on the fellas. To my shocking surprise I see Craig sitting in a chair with his hands and feet tied with a rope. Craigs hair was in plaits, but his plaits were cut to humiliate him and placed in a bag. To be honest, I knew that thought came from Jerome because Pete always analyzed things but Jerome's negative energy clouded the atmosphere. I just finished making my CD, and a hard bang came from beyond the door. "Who is it?" I asked, from the other side of the door yelled, "Police? Open up!"

This is when I knew that "All Hell was about to break loose." I opened the door and there were five officers coming in with their guns drawn. They asked, "Who's in this house?" I named everyone and told them exactly where they were. We didn't need any more surprises; especially a fatality over a mistake. I asked the police, "What address were they looking for?" They gave me the incorrect address at first.

It was from that moment I knew that we had been setup by Craig and the detectives in order to limit Kurt's help.

This was serious business because now my freedom is being compromised. The police took me, Jerome, and Pete down to the precinct. When we arrived at the precinct, our female friend, who was a lawyer, was handcuffed and sitting in a chair. I thought it was a big joke at first and I was waiting to hear "April Fools", even though it was December.

Could it have happened at a better time in my life? Three days before Christmas and we're being arrested. I asked Tina (handcuffed attorney), "What the hell is going on?" She said, "Apparently Craig was roughed up pretty bad. You know it's funny that the police never called for an ambulance, but he was supposed to be roughed up." She began to tell us that this was a plot by both police departments to have everyone incarcerated to make you guys out to have a bad reputation, and to make sure they get a conviction on your brother. We were placed in the cell and charged with "Aggravated Assault", in Philadelphia.

I guess one would ask, "What does this have to do with Bishops Need Love Too?" Well, this is breaking the foundation to allow people to see that even in the midst of turmoil, hell, opposition and negativity; one still needs to find "Love" somewhere in the atmosphere.

When you're going through hardships and it is almost impossible to see a clear pathway out.

Who can you depend on? When you're incarcerated and sent to the hole, who can you depend on? When you've done nothing wrong, but a lie sends you to prison indefinitely, who can you depend on? I want you to place yourselves within this scenario and answer: Who can you depend on?

Who can "I" depend on? This is a question that many people face in this day and time. Through opposition or adversity, WHO can I depend on? When I need someone to talk to, who can I depend on? When I'm stressed out, depressed and on the edge of committing suicide, who can I depend on? When I've lost my source of income and need help, who can I depend on? When there's no gas in the car and the school calls and tells me my child has been rushed to the hospital and I need to get there as soon as possible, who can I depend on? When I'm about to lose my home and the next step is a homeless shelter, who can I depend on? I know I have FAMILY that know, see and understand; I know I have FRIENDS that knows, hear it, and understand it, but who can I depend on? I know some will say, "They've learned to trust in Jesus, they've learned to depend on God?"

Still I ask, "Who can I depend on?" In the moment of intensity, I could only depend on ME, MYSELF, and I. I've learned that MY LIFE, is all that it says and that I have OWNERSHIP! I MUST CREATE and GENERATE MY SOURCE, instead of RELYING/ RESORTING/DEPENDING on a RESOURCE.

If MY OUTLETS are depressing then my OUTLOOK is blurred; therefore, my VISION is impaired. "I can do all things through Christ..." simply means, "I HAVE THE POWER WITHIN MY CONSCIENCE TO MAKE THE NECESSARY DECISIONS TO ACHIEVE ANYTHING IN MY LIFE!" I don't have to get permission, I don't have to wait for anyone, I don't need a prophet/ prophetess, psychic, fortune teller, witch doctor, preacher/pastor, soothsayer, family member, and friend. THIS IS MY JOURNEY,

MY EXPERIENCE, AND MY DECISIONS THAT'S CREATING MY DESTINY! – Lamont Bershawn.

The police came to get us out of the jail, but only to transfer us to the Montgomery County Correctional Facility (MCCF). Philadelphia, no longer had jurisdiction over our case. I wondered how they could do that. Wherever a crime or incident takes place, is where the defendant must be tried. In other words, in order for us to be transferred, there had to have been a kidnapping take place. What do you know; we get from Philadelphia where there was only an "Aggravated Assault" charge to twelve other charges being added. The most serious of them being "Kidnapping."

Here I am, actually incarcerated on a lie. To make things worse, we were placed on medium maximum security. This is where they put those who were charged or convicted of murder, or any other heinous crime. There were three different pods or sections per area, but each pod could see the new inmates as they came in.

And I walked towards my cell I see Kurt in his pod. I looked him in the eye, if his expression could speak, it would have said, "What the fuck are you doing in here dressed in this red jump suit?"

It was the most humiliating, yet humbling point in my life. I would not have wished this experience on my worst enemy. I was upset, angry, and pissed off with myself that I allowed myself to be caught up in this situation.

I began thinking, "Had I gone to church with my mother, I wouldn't be in this situation." It was entirely too late for that thought, but as they say, "Hind sight is 20/20."

We were all separated the time of our arrival to MCCF. People involved in the same case are never housed in the same cell or pod, neither are family members.

During the arraignment, our charges were being read by the magistrate and she put Pete, Jerome, and me on $500,000.00 cash bail (not bond) each. She also gave us the maximum time before our preliminary hearing, which happened to be two months. I had to deal with the consequences of the actions of the "Person" that I knew didn't use their brain, but I allowed myself to be used as shield to prevent this "Person" from doing hard time. Isn't that what family is supposed to do? I'm not a "Rat", so I decided to bite the bullet and walk this slap on the wrist off. I knew eventually, I'd be getting out of this situation soon.

Sometimes one MUST ask self, "How many weeds are in my garden?" We begin to get comfortable with the things that are happening around us, that we begin to lose focus on the true beauty of life and its gifts. YOUR life, YOUR space, YOUR atmosphere is what you CREATE it to be and the beauty thereof. It's time to reevaluate those plants, the flowers, the herbs within YOUR garden. The time is now to uproot those "Negative" seeds or weeds that are choking the life out of YOUR existence. In other words, there are a few weeds living in YOUR garden that have imposed and have infiltrated YOUR comfort zone. BEWARE: The weeds are there acting and playing the part, awaiting the opportune time to destroy you and what you stand for! (GET TO KNOW THE PEOPLE IN YOUR CAMP)!!
-Lamont Bershawn.

I didn't get comfortable, nor was I going to allow myself to adjust to this type of living. I must say, "I met a lot of interesting people while I was incarcerated." I didn't make friends, nor was I going to make any enemies. I was just waiting this "Nightmare" to end. I'd wake up in the morning reading the Bible, and go to sleep doing the same. Every morning I'd wake up studying. This one brother approached me and began asking me Biblical questions that he didn't understand. I didn't want to discourage him, so I encouraged him just as any preacher would. I mean, I didn't want to destroy his hope or his belief that God was going to come and set him free. To occupy time, some brothers would play pinochle, spades, tonk, or bid whist, all which happen to be card games.

Finally, the day of the preliminary hearing had come. We arrive in at the courthouse full of people wanting to hear our case. To be totally honest, our attorneys proved to the entire court room that we had been lied on.

Every detective and police officer in the room laughed at Craig, but the Magistrate received her orders to send this case to trial. This is when "All Hell began to break loose."

The prosecutor suggested that our bail was too low because in his eyes we were a menace to society. She knew in her heart that the decision she was about to make to send this case to trial was wrong. I could see it in her expression. That's probably why she didn't raise our bail.

Periodically, I would call home to check on things, but I limited calling home because I knew both of my brothers were calling too. My parents would visit us every week, but I could see that the situation was taking a toll on them. I mean, not one but all three of their children incarcerated.

There was only one visit that I really hated and that was the time my cousin came along with my father. The entire visit took place with us looking through a glass and picking up a telephone. My father made a statement, "When you guys are set free; you should allow your cousin to take you under his wing." I was humble, yet my thoughts were, "You have the audacity to say he'll take us under his wing? That mother fucker isn't perfect by a long shot. His shit just got swept under the rug, and had a gag order."

Allow me to walk you through some of the situations, to show you that I'm not the bad guy. You'll get a better glimpse and receive a better understanding as to the reason why I don't deal with certain people. There are just some people that you have to disconnect from because you know without a doubt, sooner or later "All Hell is going to break loose" or trouble is in the near future.

I always believed that God would cause a change in Jerome's life, but I learned that it wasn't so much about God making a change in him, but that I continued to distance myself from dramatic people. I was beginning to be looked upon as the conceited person, the person that didn't want to be around certain people, the person that thought he was too good to hang out and the person that thought he was better than others.

Little did they know, I never thought any of those things? I just made up within my mind that I had my very own identity; therefore, I wasn't going to be looked upon as a follower or in the shadow of another. I guess I was so focused on trying to be liked that I wasn't being real with myself.

You have to understand that you're going to do what seems most important to you at that time and initially you want to be liked, but after you get around atmospheres for a period of time you can't fake it anymore.

I had gotten so fed up that I began saying, "I don't care if they don't like me. I've got to be real with myself for me; if I keep acting like this, I'm going to lose me and if I lose me, they'll never be able to find me because they never met me; they only met what I conformed to."

I asked my mother, "How did we treat each other when we were growing up?" She said, "You've always been my different child." I asked, "What do you mean mom?" She said, "You would always be the one to make sure I was alright. If I had been away from your sight for long periods of time, you'd stop what you were doing to look for me." I remember, I'd put you guys in the play pen, and give you your snacks. You would always make sure your brother had his too. He would step on your head to get out of the play pen, but you would cover him up with your blanket while he slept. If he had eaten all of his snacks, you would share yours with him; you were the more mature youngest."

After hearing the stories of my mother's recollected thoughts, it seemed that I was the older brother for a reason. I still didn't understand in full what it was he had against me. I began to wonder, "Was it something he personally had against me?" or "Was he fighting with himself, trying to believe or live up to the lies he'd told?" I believe I hit the nail on its head. When a person is a habitual liar, they tend to believe the lies they tell and in turn try to make those lies their reality. I began to rewind to certain things that took place in our lives.

I believe Jerome became so infatuated with wanting to become a police officer because his best friend was at the brink of becoming a police officer. His best friend had two weeks left before he would be graduating from the Police Academy, but Jerome caused him to get kicked out of the Police Academy for several reasons. One reason was because Jerome was jealous of his best friend, because he couldn't become an officer because of his tarnished record. You know the old saying, "Misery loves company." An altercation transpired at his best friend's home, but Jerome pulled his best friend's girlfriend aside and told her to file a PFA or "Protection from Abuse" Order on him. It's the very thing that got his best friend kicked out of the Academy. Jerome would tell every woman he would meet that he worked for the Housing Police.

When people threw rocks, bricks, cinder blocks and stones at you in order to bruise or hurt you; you remained fearless.

When people stabbed you in your back in order to give you a fatal blow; you disinfected the cut, stitched it up and kept progressing; you remained fearless.

When people took aim at you with their "hollow point bullets" and began shooting from the hip, you leaped out of the way only to find out you became wounded but it wasn't fatal and you'd live. You remained fearless.

When that relationship/ marriage drained every ounce of love, effort and desire out of you. Your heart needed life support, your body needed rest and your mind needed to stay focused. Your life was renewed and you still remained fearless.

When that family member spewed lies on you and "dashed you with gasoline" in order to burn you alive; they didn't know that your clothing was made of "polybenzimidazole" {PBI}. You didn't flinch; you remained fearless.

When your friend or confidant became your Judas in order to betray you. The situation had the "boomerang effect." Your eyes became opened and your vision became extremely clearer to your surroundings. You remained fearless.

When that job or career laid you off. You were forced in "hellified" situations that almost drowned you. You quickly grabbed the "life raft" carrying the "wet suit" and floated to "land." Ut oh, that didn't stop you neither. You still remained fearless.

When they thought you were "suicidal" and thought you had "low self-esteem" they prescribed medication that would either keep you sleep or relaxed. They were preparing you for the "Insane Asylum." You proved them wrong on many levels until they promoted you to the status of a "genius" and began looking at those "whistle blowers, naysayers and haters" with the "side-eye." You still remained fearless.

When you left the church or your religious affiliations because you recognized the "God" within you differed from the "God" you were being taught. You were blasphemed and ostracized. You were "being nailed to their crucifix" and thrown inside their "tomb." A few hours later a few of your real friends or "roots" rescued you, cared for you and got you back on your feet. A few days later your resurrection stunned the religious world. Why? They thought you were dead, but the "Living God" had the "ram in the bush." You still remained fearless!

POINT: whatever someone says about you, does to you or do for you in order to try their best to assassinate your character or reputation is short lived. Everything that becomes conflicting or contrary to you will need life support because NOTHING can withstand YOUR power.

{Let me say it another way because someone missed it}!!!

The enemy did everything in their power to "ground" you or "kill" you. What the enemy didn't know is that you have "real friends, real family and real folk" on your behalf that are protecting, aiding and assisting you in order to help keep you focused.

This is why people that enter your life and try to be with you on a daily basis can't remain long because contrary, conniving and conflicting folk can't stand in your powerful presence. They get mad, upset and angry because what conquered others CAN'T conquer you because you're a "different breed." – Lamont Bershawn.

To be honest, we had a teacher that was also a Captain at the Housing Police, and Jerome looked up to him. Our teacher was married, but he was also a ladies' man, drove a Mercedes like my father, enjoyed drinking VO, (Scotch), loved to hang in the clubs, and belonged to the Masonic Order.

I will never forget the time Jerome went out of town with this female Correctional Officer. She believed my brother was a Police Officer.

He used to work as a Security Officer for the School Board at one time, but he was fired.

During their trip, he was caught speeding. When the Trooper arrived to the car, instead of handing his Driver's License, he showed the Trooper a fake badge. The Trooper asked him, "Are you an officer?" "Yes, Sir!" my brother replied. The Trooper went to his vehicle to find out about the identification my brother showed him. The police surrounded the vehicle, confiscated his pistol, and took him to jail.

My parents received a call that my brother had been detained and arrested for "Impersonating an Officer." My mother and Uncle Tim drove down to post bail. He had to return a few months later. My father said, "I'm not going to Maryland and I'm not giving a dime for his legal issues." His lawyer was a well-known, retired Judge. In my opinion, that's why he beat the charge.

In 1998, Jerome and I were supposed to meet my mother in Florida. My mother went to spend Mother's Day with her mother.

We decided we'd drive down to spend the time with mom and grand mom. We got into a huge argument and he threatened to kill me.

I decided that I wasn't going to ride anywhere with him. Jerome went upstairs while I called my mother to explain to her the reason I wouldn't be coming to Florida. When I got off the phone, I saw a bright light shining on the outside of the house. I went to the door to see what it was; it was the police with their guns drawn towards me telling me to come outside with my hands up.

I found out that it was Jerome who went upstairs to call the cops to tell them I threatened to kill him, when in fact those were his words to me. I went to jail that night and spent fourteen hours there.

I could not believe my brother; Jerome would actually tell a lie on me that could have turned out for the worst.

When the police had me in handcuffs, Jerome ran out of the house yelling, "He put his gun in the trunk of his car. It's in the red bag."

The cops retrieved the unloaded gun, but the bullets were locked up inside of the glove compartment. When the detective began finger printing me, he said, "You don't have to tell me anything, but I know your brother told a fucking lie on you. Does your brother know that you could have been killed, because the arriving officers looked for you to have a gun on your possession? Any false or reactionary move would've cost you your life."

I posted my own bail the next morning. During the Preliminary Hearing, the Judge dismissed the case.

I went to the police station where they gave me my pistol back and I headed home. My mother and my Uncle Tim were in court with me. On our way home, I told my mother, "Jerome was going to either get someone killed, or cause someone to spend a very long time behind bars."

Anyone that's labeled an "accomplished" or habitual liar that goes to the extent of not only believing his own lie but invests in it is extremely dangerous.

Lamont Bershawn

I literally had to LEGALLY drop my last name because our name was similar {same DOB, initials, similar SSN and photo}. I got tired of making positive moves and being "red flagged." I had to always carry a letter from the PA. State Police verifying my identity because he kept involving himself in stupid shit.

Years ago, many people have told me that he was jealous/ envious of me, but in my mind... he's my brother.

It never dawned on me how dangerous he was until 2003, when he made a negative statement to law enforcement concerning my oldest brother who was on trial for murder.

He blames me for everything negatively taking place in his life {his insecurities, inconsistencies, him becoming a CONVICTED FELON, his breakups, etc.}. No one made him buy a FAKE DEGREE using YOUNGSFIELD UNIVERSITY {FAKE UNIVERSITY}, receiving a Bachelors in "Criminal Justice" and a Masters in "Chiropractic Science."

He did a radio interview a few days ago lying through his teeth. I have tried to encourage him to do things the correct way. I've also told him a number of times that if an individual can't accept you for who you are, leave them alone. If you have to lie or put on a mask to be accepted by those you consider a "friend", they're not worth the foundation your lie sits upon.

A few weeks ago, I was asked to watch the movie, "The Dark Mirror." It was about a set of twins {one good and the other evil.}. The evil twin ended up killing the good twin and began living her life as the good one.

I had to make this post for a few reasons: to protect my identity, protect my reputation/ character and to reveal the truth. He even created a FAKE BADGE with a bar code. He has a list of criminal activity, yet he'd like people to believe it's me.

If you're his friend, YOUR LIVELIHOOD, YOUR REPUTATION, YOUR CHARACTER, YOUR BELONGINGS AND YOU ARE IN THE MIDST OF A DEADLY and DANGEROUS PERSON! – Lamont Bershawn #youhavenoideawhatitfeelslikebeingatwin

I knew it would be best for me to move out of the state, so I moved to Florida. My job had an opening, so I left. When I arrived in Florida, I considered it a new beginning. I worked for CLS (Central Locating Service) in the morning and became head of "Public Safety" at JU (Jacksonville University) in the evening. I had my own place, was doing well and things were beginning to prosper for me.

A few months passed, Jerome and I were on speaking terms once again. He came to visit me. I told him to make himself at home, but in the morning time, he would visit my grandparents and when I got off work, I'd pick him up.

One evening, I allowed him to come to work with me at JU. An incident took place, Jerome decided to try to pick a fight with one of the students. My boss found out the next morning, what transpired, I was called in and fired. It was my duty to protect the students and faculty. I did take control of the situation at the scene, but because I was Black and the head of Public Safety (beating out five others for the position), it was leverage for me to lose my position.

In 2007, Jerome and his girlfriend went to Atlantic City for the weekend. "All Hell breaks loose" in their hotel room this particular weekend. They're cussing and arguing. Both had been under the influence of alcohol, but she received a call from her mother that she needed to get home immediately. My brother told her they needed to get rest. He wasn't about to get behind the wheel of the car intoxicated. She felt the need to go down to security to tell them that "her ex-boyfriend came down and found out where she was; now he's holding her against her will."

Security looks at her like she's crazy and says, "If he's holding you against your will, how are you speaking with me?" She said, "I left when I saw him pulling out his gun." Security immediately calls the police. The police arrive up to the room and asked everyone to get on the floor. They asked for my brother, but he'd already caught the elevator with his bag in his hand. The police called down to their partners who were in the lobby. They saw him on the camera as he made his way to the lobby via the elevator. As soon as he walked off the elevator the police (guns drawn) said, "Place the bag on the floor and place both hands behind your head. Continue to walk backwards holding both hands on your head.

When they detained him, she began to look at him with a smile on her face. He was taken to jail. He couldn't reach either of my parents, so he called me on my cell phone collect. I asked, "Why is he calling me collect?" The operator said, "He's calling from Atlantic County jail, will you accept the charges and how are you going to pay?" I declined and called my parents. He knew only Federal, State and Local agents were the only officers allowed to carry firearms on casino properties, but that was example of the foolish chances that he takes.

In 2008, Jerome cut the brake line to my "Adopted" Uncle's vehicle because he was angry at the things he said about my mother. My "Adopted" Uncle and I had a bad track record and didn't get along because he thought he could control everybody. I actually saw my brother cut the brake line, but I never said anything about it to anyone.

The next morning, I received a call from Bucks a County police detective. He asked me about the incident. I told him I had no idea what he was talking about. Again, I wasn't about to "Rat" on Jerome. My parents were dealing with enough; they didn't need another son incarcerated again. I mean it would've been his fifth time.

The detective said my Uncle told him that he saw me leaving the premises. I laughed and told the officer, "Believe me, if he would've seen me at that house, he wouldn't have hesitated to call you guys."

Misery

A few days later, the sheriff came to my house and served me "Protection Order" papers. So, I had to appear in court. Here I am, once again brought into another situation because of Jerome. My attorney and his attorney made an agreement that I would have to call 24 hours in advance because he was living in their home. In order for me to see my grandparents I also had to come with my mother.

I now had a "Protection from abuse" Order that would be in effect for three years. I refused to be placed on a leash like a dog in order to see my grandparents, so I didn't go back until the day before my grandmother died on June 29, 2009.

This was the straw that broke the camel's back. I had once again allowed Jerome to infiltrate in on my stability, my happiness, my joy, my money and my life. I was unemployed for a few days, before I landed a job at "Bermex", contracting company reading electric and water meters for the city.

I was very concerned about my life and the direction I was headed. I wasn't doing anything that would cause years of delay, but I was very concerned with the things I allowed people to do because of the love I have for them. I reached out to a mutual friend of the family, who didn't have anything to lose or gain by being truthful.

This person knew my family for years and practically saw us grow up. I met up with Damon and asked him his view or perception of Jerome and me.

What he said shocked me because certain things he said I thought I was the only one aware of them. Damon went on to say, "You two look similar, but you're like night and day. One of you should have been a girl." "Huh?" I replied. "Yep, Jerome has been jealous of you for years. He's an opportunist that preys on the less fortunate to gain wealth. When it comes to loyalty, he has none."

As Damon was speaking, I was all ears because it was confirming the things I felt. I began looking back at situations we were in, the situation involving he and his best friend, the musical groups where he betrayed the person that got him involved to begin with, former female friends who also told me that he propositioned them. This was truly an awakening moment that let me know that I wasn't the problem after all.

Moments after the conversation Damon said something to me that was very profound. First Damon said, "Lamont, you're very brilliant and I was wondering if you would ever notice your own intellectual mind. I'll never forget the first time I came to hear you preach on New Year's Eve. It was a message that I felt set you free of the obstacles you were dealing with and I too felt liberated." Damon said to always remember this, "A snake never mourns the loss of its shredded skin." In other words, there are things in life that will grow on you, but when they become a hindrance you must learn to shed the weight and keep on moving forward.

When Kurt was going through his murder trial, Jerome made a negative written statement to the detectives that if it were used could have destroyed his chance of getting an innocent verdict. He was found guilty, but it wasn't because of the evidence in the case.

Did I do something wrong? Was I being punished for doing, or not doing something? I was still preaching. I began looking for a church home. I began attending, "First Baptist of Mandarin." My mother called me and said, "Why don't you join one of the sister churches located in Florida."

One Sunday I decided to go. I sat down in the pew. An older lady walked up to me and said, "You're a preacher, aren't you?" I replied, "Yes ma'am." She took me by the hand and ushered me into the pulpit.

There weren't many people in the church on this particular day, but it was a handful. The regular pastor was out of town and the visiting Pastor became ill. Was this a coincidence and I'm present or was this designed by God?

Nevertheless, they asked me if I would bring the message. I preached on that Sunday and it was awesome.

The musician took my information and asked me to come back to fellowship with them, I felt right at home. I told them where I came from in Philadelphia. They remembered my mother and couldn't wait to call her to tell her how wonderful of a job I had done. Once again, my life was on the correct path or track. I was doing well and landed another job working for Pepsi Cola.

I didn't have time to focus on the negative things, so I began meditating on my life. I began thinking seriously about the choices I made, the people I allowed to be in my company, the things I took for granted and the people who looked up to me as a mentor. There were a number of mistakes and errors that I made in my life, but never anything that would land me in jail.

I thought about the times I was blamed for something that I didn't do, the times I was ridiculed and the times I had been passive just for peace sake. Well, the "Passive" Lamont was about to perish because at that moment, I promised myself that I would never be passive or keep quiet again especially if this is a result of allowing God to handle it. I was always taught to allow God to fight my battles, but I had been incarcerated now for almost three months. Evidently, this was one of the battles that God decided to sit out on.

On Friday, March 21, 2003, my brother and I had a bail hearing. There were over fifty people sitting in the court room on our behalf. The Judge received a number of letters from prominent people, speaking on our behalf. When we arrived at court, I was wondering why Pete wasn't there. The attorneys felt it would be a wise decision to sever our case from Pete's, because Pete had a sixty-five-page rap sheet. Our bail was dropped from $1,000,000 cash (combined) to $100,000 cash (combined).

My parents paid the $100,000 cash, court dismissed late in the day, so the transactions took place on Monday, March 24, 2003. Jerome and I were released around 3:00 p.m. It was one of the best moments in my life. I felt bad for Pete because he should have been released along with us, but my parents' legal battles were just beginning. The situation with us being free, but Pete still incarcerated brought negative feelings towards us from Pete. I understood, believe me!!

I often heard that, "Everything happened for a reason, in its very own season." I began looking at this situation a few different ways. Was this part of God's plan, in order to bring my family closer together? Was this my final wake up call to finally accept what I saw in people, and stop giving them the benefit of doubt? Did this happen so that I could see exactly who my true friends and family are?

Reality: Growing up I really didn't understand the value of things, but I'm thankful for parents who looked beyond the present into the future and for longevity. What I've come to understand is you'll truly find out who has your best interest at heart when a tough situation arises. This is when you'll see the "Sheep scatter." This is a test that is DEFINITELY needed because we (as people) become so comfortable being a part of crowds that we really don't know who's genuine and who's an imposter, or an intruder. While going through the "Storm", you will determine who they are by their offer. "If" people come and offer (1) prayer - these are the people (a) who really would like to help (b) who are a part of the broke, busted and disgusted (ain't got shit), (c) who really don't want to help, but want you to think they do; (2) Jesus - these are those who are in DENIAL; (3) Money - these are the people who (a) either have experienced something similar and want to help (b) are true friends that trust you, knows your character and are willing to go to battle along your side!

It was this situation, this moment in my life that I realized that my father loved me. Sometimes it's hard for people to express their love for you because your perception of love may differ from theirs. What I've come to notice and understand is that there are many different categories and facets of love. It's not always easy to show affection towards someone if there's embedded hurt that a person's still carrying from their past. Some people are neglected, given up for adoption, experience mental/emotional abuse from the individual that tells them they love them.

Whatever the case, when a person loves themselves their interpretation of "The love they have come to know", must match the "love" of the one they intend on connecting with.

"God is Love, Love is Perfect and since YOU'RE in the image thereof: It means you're perfect. POINT: Stop trying to connect with people that are contrary to YOUR spirit. Opposites don't always attract!" - Lamont Bershawn.

I had to walk you through a portion of my journey, so that you could better understand the person who made daily though provoking Facebook posts, has become a very humbled man, and have come to be mindful of other people's personal experiences.

"The individual that you see daily, converse with over the phone, are friends with, dislike for whatever reason are products of a struggle that YOU have no idea of. Be mindful of the judgments YOU'RE making about a person. What they have made it through, could have been the very thing that killed you!!" - Lamont Bershawn.

It had only been a week that I was released from being incarcerated. I spent a total of ninety- four days incarcerated because of a lie. I made the decision to go to Florida to see my grandparents, because I knew she was worried, concerned and hadn't seen me in three months. When I arrived, my grandmother hugged me and started to cry. I told her that I was okay, just glad to be out. I showered, got dressed and relaxed for a while just getting caught up in the moment of appreciating life and freedom.

My grandmother, being a "Spiritualist" looked over at me and said, "I know what happened?" I asked, "What do you mean, you know what happened?" She said, "The reason you were incarcerated." In the beginning I felt relieved, but then I asked her, "Well, tell me what happened?" I really just wanted her to prove to me, how much of a "Spiritualist" she was.

She responded with, "You all beat the shit out of that young man and humiliated him." I was shocked to say the least at her response. I immediately responded and said, "With all due respect, if you don't know what happened the best thing to do is to shut the fuck up. I spent ninety- four days incarcerated on some shit that had nothing to do with me and you have the audacity to tell me WE whooped his ass as well as humiliated him." I said,

"I apologize for the language I just used, but what's surprising to me is that you have seen me grow from a little boy into a man; you've attended the churches to hear me preach; you've watched my work ethics; how I became an intercessor for my mother; you've seen me give up what little I had to bless those that were less fortunate. I'm sold into believing that you never knew me, but it was a front all along to compensate with us for the times you've missed out on your very own daughter's life."

One thing I'll never forget as long as I live is that you told me, "The two adopted children will always be more of your children, than my mother ever would be." I had never experienced the exchanging of words like that ever with my grandmother.

I left to get some fresh air, so I went to the bowling alley. I didn't bowl, but I saw a few people that I used to bowl on a league with. They came up to me and said, "They were sorry to hear what happened." I said, "Thanks." I didn't know, nor at the moment did I really care if anyone's perception of me had changed. I returned back to my grandmother's house, told her that I still loved her and I was sorry for the things I said. She said, "It's okay, I understand." My grandmother never was one to say, "I'm sorry" or "She was wrong." The way you knew that she knew she was wrong is because she'd buy you something and take you to get a bite to eat.

The next morning, I got up and washed the car. It was a 1979 Cadillac Fleetwood, still in good condition. I saw my grandmother peeking out of the window. When I got back in the house I showered and got dressed. My grandmother said, "Let's go get something to eat." We went to a restaurant called, "Piccadilly." I just loved their carrot souffle, it tasted a lot like my mother's sweet potato pie. When we left there, to my surprise, we went to the Nissan dealership. She said, "Look around and let me know if you see something you like?"

There was a new Maxima, that was the anniversary series that I liked a lot, but the price was $30,000. When I looked over, there was a black on black Maxima, with tinted windows, and a spoiler. It wasn't brand new, but it was very sharp and clean. I told my grandmother that I liked it. To make a long story short, I drove that black Maxima off the lot. It was my grandmother's way of saying, "I'm sorry." It was also her way of showing you how much she really appreciated you. I heard the disappointment through the things my grandmother said, yet she expressed how much she still was in my corner through her actions.

I drove to Philadelphia the following weekend because the following Wednesday, we had to appear in court. Our case wasn't yet over, remember, we were out on bail. Each time we'd appear in court, the case would be continued. The case was continued for a year and a half. We, (Jerome and I) settled on making a deal. We accepted a guilty plea of one count of "Simple Assault" with non-reported probation of two years. I would apply for different jobs and would pass the test to get in, but every time they had to rescind on their offer due to my criminal background check.

"A layoff notice is NOT a termination notice; it's just a notice that states, you're too qualified for THIS position and you became too comfortable in it so I'm giving you the opportunity to excel and use the talents God possessed within you. They've been dormant far too long, and now it's time for YOUR gifts to make room for you!!" -Lamont Bershawn.

I began working under the table, but it really wasn't helping me much, so I decided to go to North Carolina to work for my cousin because he owned his own concrete company. I became a brick layer and came to the conclusion that being in the hot sun, lifting and handling brick wasn't the best thing for me. My mom owns a home in North Carolina, so that's where I was staying. My other Uncle found out I was in town, so I began helping him hang drywall. It was a better environment and I didn't have to worry about hot brick or getting burned. I wasn't afraid of hard work at all. Actually, I didn't think anything got accomplished if I wasn't dirty or sweating profusely.

Business became slow, so I found myself back in Pennsylvania.

I got to Pennsylvania; my parents were in their room having a conversation about us. My mother believed that God was testing the family, and would make a way soon. I really didn't know my father's thoughts. He never openly spoke about it, but I could imagine how the conversations went with his friends. They're speaking about their children's accomplishments, but if he had to say something it would've been, "Well, Kurt is in prison for murder; Lamont just got out of jail and he's still a preacher; Jerome also just got out of jail and he's teaching martial arts; and I have a daughter outside of my marriage who's in school becoming a doctor."

Sometimes I wonder if my father thinks he failed in raising his male children. Sometimes I wonder if he set us up to be failures in his eyes. Sometimes I wonder if he never wanted a connection to his male children because he had a much better connection to his nephews opposed to his very own sons. Was he disappointed? Did he really regret having us with my mother? Were we neglected in a sense because we had a loving mother and grandmother?

When one can take the power of other individuals thought, mindset, or conscience in order to lead them into darkness from their OWN marvelous light, it makes them a slave because they'd rather ACCEPT another person's vision and neglect/ deny their OWN. My vision is NOT your vision; My interpretation/ perception is NOT yours; My ways, thoughts, experiences, trials, tribulations, mistakes, mishaps are some of the important occurrences that have made and molded me into the person YOU see on this day. POINT: When I was a child, I thought like a child, I reasoned like a child, I acted/ behaved like a child, I listened/ obeyed like a child and yes, I was even chastised like a child; but when I became a MAN, I put aside my childish ways, thoughts. To begin THINKING for MYSELF!! I've learned to take the negative and see the positive through it; I've taken the lemons to make lemonade; I've taken the cards I've been dealt to create a winning hand; and I've taken my negative past to create a positive and more influential future.

You're more than a conqueror, you're a GOD and YOU OWN YOUR MOMENTS!! -*Lamont Bershawn.*

When I would sit back and begin to reflect on my childhood, it was a fairly decent one. I can only go by my thoughts, my interpretation, and my perception of the things I had gone through. It's not to say that someone else didn't have a better life than I had, nor is it to say that someone had a much worse experience. All I knew is that I had to bring a positive outcome through the negative thoughts I had. I brought myself to reason with me. In other words, not the developed thoughts or perception those others taught me to have, but the thoughts that I personally developed.

The greatest relief I received was when I stopped playing the "Blame" game and started to take responsibility for my own actions. Why was I ever incarcerated? It was because I allowed a negative person to bring me into a negative situation, thinking that I could shield and protect them, but refused to govern myself. I'm constantly reminded that I must take care of the "Star" player. No one's going to watch my back or protect me better than me, take good care of me, better than me, make sure I have what I need, better than me. I started to watch movies, listen to music, read books that enhanced my spirit, my belief, and my level of thought. I began to hang around people that could deposit an "Inspirational" word into my spirit, people that uplifted me instead of tearing me down. People that would encourage me instead of telling me, "I would never become anything." In other words, I came to understand me and stopped believing other people's perception of me.

I constantly hear people say, "As long as you place God first in all you do, everything will fall into place." Well, first and foremost when one places themselves first, you're also placing God first. Anyone who has ever been on an airplane know/ understands and receives instructions from the flight attendant, "In the case of an emergency the masks will fall from the above compartment. Please place mask on SELF before aiding another." One could also believe

that God will send you through a series of tests before going to the next level. This is what W.A.I.T. means as in "Wait I say on the Lord." (Wilderness, Alone, Increase, Test). I'm going to place you in the "Wilderness" (state of mind) "Alone." While you're there I'm going to "Increase" your tenacity, knowledge, understanding and your value. So, when I place you back into the world amongst the people, you'll be able to withstand any "Test."

POINT: Remember to ALWAYS take care of the STAR PLAYER (SELF); Your Mind, Body, and Spirit. Do that and you'll realize that you've been placing God 1st!! God still NEEDS people to do the "Footwork". Keep yourself Healthy and people will begin to see the God in/ through you (mirror image of self)!! - *Lamont Bershawn.*

Kurt sent a couple of DVD's home that the prison allowed him to partake in. They were very nice and inspirational. When the DVD came on, it was a nice song playing, and my brother sitting in a chair with a selected family portrait as his background.

On the DVD was him giving his breakdown or interpretation of selected Biblical scripture. I believe this opened the door for my parent's to finally see where my belief was, because I had questions but they didn't have any answers. I wondered, "Do people go to church with so many questions, but because most can't come in contact with their Pastor, their questions go unanswered?" On the DVD, my brother asked everyone to stretch their hands in "Faith" towards the television for their healing and his release. My mother asked me, "Are you going to stretch your hands in faith towards the television?" I said, "Of course not."

When the video went off, I asked my parents, "How long have you been praying for his release?" He's been incarcerated almost ten years. So many people have passed away, his daughter is about to graduate middle school, his appeals are getting denied, and you constantly keep his name on the church prayer bulletin. How long will you continue with believing that God has him incarcerated for a reason? How long will you tell yourselves and others that in God's time he will be released? If you really believe that it's all about God's timing, don't hire another attorney and waste your money. They both looked at me as if I struck a nerve, but I could tell what I said to them triggered some thought.

I told them, "Here we are expected to be a family, but aren't on one accord." I asked my parents, "Have you ever wondered why, we as brothers had a problem with getting along at times?" My father responded, "You guys are grown and make your own decisions." I explained to him, "Part of the reason behind our relationship as brothers had a lot to do with the way we saw you treat mom, and the way you chose to connect with your brothers. Our Kurt treated his friends better than he treated us, but only one of his friends attended his trial. Only one of his friends placed money on his books. The superficial friends that he collected along the way, when they needed something were nowhere to be found."

Remember the saying, "Charity starts at home and is spread abroad." In this household it's different. It's more like, "Charity starts on the streets and is never to be brought home."

My father looked at me as if I hit the jugular vein with a knife. I knew it was too much that I said at one time, but it was time for change to happen. My father walked up to his room and closed the door. Later that evening, my mother approached me and said, "The things you've brought to your father's attention made him cry." I didn't intend on making anyone cry, I just wanted them to know what I'd been carrying for so long and at a young age I understood what was going on.

The next day my father came into my room and we talked. In the beginning, I was a little nervous because I didn't know exactly what to expect. The first thing he did was hug me. It was at that point that I knew within my heart that my father really cared he just wasn't used to expressing his love. I often wondered was my paternal grandfather strict to the point he really didn't take time out to express his love for his very own children. Sometimes things become hereditary or passed through the generations. All habits, curses, spells, or patterns can easily be broken but only if they are recognized.

In this moment of my life, I see things differently or for a better term, I can see clearly now. When we're so prone to making final judgments on others based off what we've heard, seen, or personally experienced it allows people to shut down. Notice the moment you say, "Hello" to another person what you're dealing with. You've just begun to experience that individuals train of thought, every person who ever rejected them, every teacher that ever taught them something, their parents train of thought, every person that ever lied on them, every sexual experience, everyone who planted negative seeds, every person who had their back and then decided to fold. from the moment you say, "Hello."

I've had my trials and tribulations, but the greatest achievement is learning from my personal experience through this journey called life. No one ever really loses, no one ever really wins because it's all personal and has been assigned to you from the moment you came through your mother's womb. I've learned to stop playing the "Blame" game and decided to take responsibility for my life and my actions to produce results.

Stop playing the "Blame" game! To my brothers and sisters, it has been brought to my attention that some of us are still playing the "Blame" game or the race card. We must educate our children and stop teaching or allowing them to wind up behind the "Eight Ball." Churches and Prisons are two institutions that are constantly growing and are backed by the state to help them govern the population. These places will never lose their accreditation as long as they continue to house those who are disabled, destitute, or mentally ill. If no one ever wondered why the church is called the hospital, it's because it's built for those who want to escape REALITY by giving their problems to an imaginary being.

The tithes and offerings NEVER go to God, but goes to the church and the pastor as a "Copay" for services rendered. The only medicine that's prescribed is "Jesus" and a little anointing oil that really has no power.

Misery

One of my friends called and said to me, "Have you lost your mind? You weren't raised that way into posting the things that you do. I can no longer be your friend until you come back to Jesus." My response: "When I was a child I acted as a child, spoke as a child, believed as a child, followed as a child and thought as a child, but when I became a man, I put away those childish things. As far as you no longer being my friend, until I come back to Jesus... It seems to me that you never got off of Jesus, but I'll NEVER go back.

We are allowing our children to grow up with the "Slave Mentality" because we're ACCEPTING the foolishness that's been handed to us and passed down through the generations.

POINT: We can no longer play the "Blame" game without being RESPONSIBLE for ourselves. There's more "black on black" crime, "black on black" murder, "black on black" enslavement. It's NOT the devil, it's NOT God, it's NOT the "Race" game, but it's prompted by the lack of self-respect, the lack of education, the lack of true mentoring.

We've ACCEPTED the Easter Bunny, Santa Clause, Tooth Fairy far too long. It's time for each of us to "Reach one, teach one in order for us to Be ONE!"–*Lamont Bershawn.*

The Enemy Poem

Who is the real enemy?
Can it be someone that's really afraid of me?
Intimidated for a reason that's unknown,
Or formed a reason on their own.

You desire to destroy my character,
All because you're a non-factor.
You've cried just to get attention,
Because your name doesn't even get mentioned.

I hate having to waste my inner-G,
On anything involving your insecurity,
I asked momma to stop holding your hand,
Or you'll never grow up and be your own man.

You've lied on me long enough,
In order to make my life tough and rough.
Brother, you see me as your enemy,
When all you did was strengthen my inner-me.

Remove the cracked glass out of the mirror,
You'll be able to see yourself much clearer.
You can still be anything you desire to be,
Just don't look at me as your enemy.
- Lamont Bershawn {Original Piece}

The Enemy Tried to Devour My Inner-Me

It was twenty-six years ago when I felt that I met my soulmate. I'll never forget it because it was a very beautiful and sunny day in North Carolina. I was standing in the front yard with my cousin enjoying the breeze when two young ladies were walking by pushing a baby stroller and carrying a couple of grocery bags. I spoke and they greeted me back. The one pushing the stroller looked back at me and smiled. I smiled back at her and immediately jogged up to her and offered to help carry her bags. I asked, "What's your name?" She kindly responded, "My name is Melissa. What's your name? My name is Lamont.

We arrived at a trailer that she shared with her cousin. She went in to drop her bags off, get her son situated and came back outside to talk with me. We took a walk to the baseball field. We laughed and talked so long that I had no idea that we spent three hours at the baseball field. Melissa looked at me and said, "You're not from around here, so where are you from?" "I'm from Philadelphia, Pennsylvania", I replied. I came down to spend a little time with my grandmother but I'll be leaving in two days. Melissa began to look into my eyes and we began to kiss. I wrapped my arms around her waist as she placed her arms around my neck and the passion behind the kiss let me know how she felt. I walked her back to her house as a gentleman should and before I could walk away, she kissed me one more time and handed me a piece of paper with her telephone number on it.

I walked back to my grandmother's house which was about three blocks away feeling like I was on cloud nine. The following morning, I called Melissa to see what her plans were. Melissa said, "I have no plans. My cousin is giving her daughter a birthday party and I'm going to be here." I really didn't have any plans; all I know is that I didn't want to leave town without seeing her again. Melissa called me after the birthday party and after about thirty minutes of talking she said that she'd like to see me before I left town.

My grandmother wanted some butter pecan ice cream from the supermarket, so I called Melissa to see if she wanted to ride with me and spend some time together. On my way to the supermarket I picked Melissa up and asked if she needed anything? She said, "No, thank you." I dropped the ice cream off to my grandmother and Melissa and I rode to the park, listened to music, talked and laughed. Melissa had a great sense of humor, athletic physique, beautiful smile, cocoa brown skin and her spirit was amazing. Neither of us wanted the night to end but I had to get my rest so I wouldn't be tired driving. When I walked Melissa to her door, she hugged and kissed me as if she didn't want me to forget her. Melissa asked me to wait one second as she went into her house. She came back outside and immediately grabbed me by the hand and walked me directly to her bedroom. Melissa said that her cousin dropped her son off at her mother's for church in the morning. Melissa was nineteen at the time and I was twenty-0ne. Melissa began kissing me as she was unbuckling my pants. She put her braids in a ponytail, disrobed and we began making love. Tears began falling from Melissa's eyes as we kissed passionately with every thrust. I asked her, "Why are you crying?" She replied, "I've never felt so connected and loved by anyone. Please don't stop!!" As we made love, I realized the condom broke as I was cumming, but the feeling was so intense that I didn't pull out. When we finished cleaning ourselves up, it was time for me to head back to my grandmothers to rest before her cousin returned home. When Melissa walked me to the door, she looked at me and said, "Promise me, you'll come back to see me?" I kissed her and said, "I promise?"

The next morning, I hit the road heading back to Pennsylvania. We called each other while I was traveling and told each other how much fun we had and missed each other. When I made it home, I called my grandmother and Melissa to let them know that I arrived safely. I had to work in the morning so I couldn't talk to Melissa all night. I received a beautiful letter a few days later from Melissa. She was letting me know that she loved and missed me terribly and that she couldn't wait until I came back down. I called Melissa to let her know that I received her letter and her phone was either off or she changed her number. Either way, I had no way of contacting her. I wrote her back and I didn't receive a response, nor did the letter come back. I was puzzled and couldn't figure out what happened.

The end of the month I drove back to North Carolina. I immediately went by her cousin's trailer but no one was there. The few people I knew in town didn't know her, so I waited patiently to see if I'd get a phone call, text or just bumped into her while I was there. Well, I didn't get a chance to see her this time but my heart still missed her. I searched social media and couldn't locate her and then I thought to myself, "If it's meant to be, we'd cross each other's paths again."

I stopped trying to reach her and I never received another letter from Melissa so I felt that I was too far away and she moved on. Either way, I wanted what's best for her even if it wasn't with me.

Six months later, I was at a church convention in Washington, D.C. and received a phone call that my cousin passed away. The ironic thing was he was a Pastor in D.C. but wasn't affiliated with my church. A week later was his home going service. I met one of his congregants named, Tammy. Tammy was petit with a beautiful smile. She was an awesome chef too. We exchanged numbers and began dating. I was working Sunday night until Friday morning. Every Friday morning when I'd get off work, I'd come home, shower and grab my clothes bag and drive to Adelphi, Maryland to see her. It was only a two-and-a-half-hour drive and it gave me something to do every weekend. Tammy was a few years older than me, was into the church and loved catering. Her mother could bake a delicious coconut cream pie, which was my favorite. We fell apart when I realized she wasn't being as faithful as I'd hoped.

A few months later, I began writing my first book and pretty much focused on writing until my Uncle's wife felt the need to introduce me to her friend's daughter. I waited until the weekend to call her and meet her. My initial thought after meeting her was, "She's attractive, but she's definitely not my type." Her entire family was very welcoming and the first thing her mother said to me was, "I believe you were sent here by God." I allowed those words to filter into my heart being as though I was entering into "religious ministry." I began dating Barbara as I placed my book on the back burner.

Barbara had a great sense of humor and was a decent and fair person. She was the person that actually helped me to stay focused and helped me stay grounded in the midst of turmoil. We developed a great friendship and we were able to talk about everything. This is what I always desired, my lady who was also considered my best friend. Eight months into our relationship I asked Barbara to marry me. She accepted the proposal and we opened a joint account and began saving for a home and preparing for a wedding. The proposal in my opinion was informal and in my heart of hearts I wanted our families to be involved, but at a later date. My job transferred me to Florida because a new facility had opened and I put in for it because Barbara and I really didn't want to live in Pennsylvania any longer, but I knew she couldn't move to Florida just yet. When I moved, I got an apartment a few weeks later and flew Barbara out so she could begin putting in her resume. A few of her friends and family members didn't want to see her leave and they seemed to have a greater influence on her than I did, so she decided to stay in Philly. We did our best to maintain a great relationship although I knew it would be a matter of time before our distance apart would be too much to deal with. We maintained a great and positive friendship and put our wedding plans on hold. I had vacation time so I drove from Florida to Philly and on my way, I stopped in North Carolina to rest at my mother's home. It was early when I got to North Carolina so I drove passed the trailer where Melissa stayed the last time, I saw her and the trailer was falling apart. I went back to my mother's house and rested a few hours before I hit the road again, heading to Philly.

When I got to Philly, I stopped by to briefly see Barbara and she was excited because I didn't tell anyone I was coming. I left Barbara's and went to my parent's home to surprise them. When I walked into the house my Doberman was standing at the top of the stairs with his ears pointed at attention, peeking around the corner to see who was tiptoeing in his home. When he saw me, his tail began wagging and he ran and jumped into my arms. I stayed in Philly longer than expected because I got a job offer paying more money at a Pharmaceutical company. Needless to say, I accepted the position and quit my job in Florida.

Now that I was back in Philly, Barbara and I started going strong again. Once, I established myself again in the workforce, I began saving money as we never stop depositing into our joint account. Two months later, I asked her family to be at my parent's home around 8pm on that Saturday. I called Barbara early Saturday morning and asked her to put on a formal dress and that I'd be there to pick her up at 5pm. She had no idea that I was picking her up in a limousine and taking her to her favorite restaurant. When I arrived at her house all of her neighbors were outside taking pictures as if we were going on a prom. When I stepped out of the car, I had a corsage that my mother made in my hand. I rang her doorbell and her family was awaiting my arrival. Barbara came downstairs and she looked stunning. We hopped into the limousine and she smiled with tears flowing from her eyes as I told her how much I missed her. We ate and headed back to my parent's house for the finale. When we arrived, cars were everywhere. Barbara asked me, "Why are so many cars at your house?" I replied, "My mother cooked dinner and invited your mom over." When we got into the house my family and her family were there and I properly proposed. When she accepted my proposal, my close friend began playing a love ballad on the piano, dedicating it to the both of us. Our night ended at the Hilton Hotel with chocolate covered strawberries and champagne.

Six months after the engagement Barbara's stepmother passed away and it hit Barbara like a ton of bricks. Her stepmother was extremely nice and enjoyed when we'd visit. She'd cook deep fried squirrel, hush puppies, homemade coleslaw and a 7up cake. When we left the funeral Barbara received another call that her favorite Uncle passed. Two deaths within two weeks hit Barbara hard and she fell into a slump that even I couldn't penetrate. Things began getting hard to deal with in our relationship and the only thing we had in common was our sexual appetite with each other. Sooner than later I realized all we had was a sexual relationship. Both of us desired more than just sex so she gave me back my ring, I dissolved our joint account and we ended our relationship.

Nine months later Barbara contacted me to see how things were going with me and she told me that she was in a relationship and pregnant. I was extremely happy for her because I knew she wanted a baby, but I wasn't ready for that type of responsibility. Barbara and I are still great friends at this very moment and she's happily married.

Here it is five years since I heard anything from Melissa. I began wondering what happened to her. Is she okay? Did she die or get in some sort of trouble? Did she get married? Did she join the convent? So many thoughts came across my mind that I began to search Google.

I saw her name on Intelius and verified her birthdate. Finally, I found something that let me know that she got into legal trouble writing bad checks and stealing. I thought to myself, "This can't be the same young lady that I made such an impression on my heart." I stopped looking for Melissa knowing that she started creating a bad track record for herself, although my heart couldn't dismiss her or the thought that something happened in her life that made her choose that path.

I finished writing my first book, "Bishops Need Love Too." I was traveling doing book signings, speaking engagements, blog talk radio interviews, webinars and becoming a household name. In my assessment, my life had just begun at the ripe age of forty.

I still didn't have any children, but the release of my book became my baby. I realized that it was up to me to make this a priority in marketing, selling, promoting and creating another pathway to opening a door, outside of religion. I knew that the odds were against me while going against the grain of religious doctrine, dogma, principles, rituals, rules, regulations and the religious organizations. I spent the next five years trying my best to get people to take their own mask off in order to deal with their true identity. In other words, I had to lead by being an example by "dying unto myself."

"Dying unto myself", meant that I had to become transparent. In order for me to be transparent, I had to be real with myself and everyone else. It meant that I had to recognize my strength as well as my weakness, my insecurities and my intuitiveness, my flaws, faults, failures and favor. It was like the life of a butterfly. The butterfly only exists when the original form of the caterpillar makes the decision to stop eating. In other words, the caterpillar begins to "fast." A "fast" according to religion is when an individual "turns down their plate" and begins to pray to "God" for a cause or an answer. It's a personal "sacrifice" to gain awareness. So, the caterpillar hangs upside down from a leaf or a twig and spins itself into a silky cocoon. In other words, the caterpillar creates its own "casket" in order to become "resurrected." During the time in the cocoon the caterpillar transforms itself into a butterfly or a moth. When we as people understand that it's imperative for us to die unto ourselves in order to fly, we'll continue to be like the worm and eat the debris from the earth or be eaten by predators.

One thing I've learned on this journey of life is that people are sometimes more comfortable telling lies, living lies or receiving lies than they are with being authentic and genuine. Why? It's because the majority will believe the lie quicker than they believe the truth, even if the truth is presented before their eyes in black and white. What I've learned is less than five percent of the world's population walk around with masks on daily. You'll be surprised with the percentage of people that deal with unresolved issues or traumatic experiences that they just don't want to remember, relive, deal with or accept. Just because they refuse to deal with it, cover it up or mask the issue doesn't mean that it's dead or gone. It means that it's been covered with dirt for protective purposes only, but like a seed it's sure to sprout up once again.

Many people try to run away from themselves and hide in the church, trying to find solace with biblical scripture or any religious organization that will reference a mediator will handle your issue or pain. Does it help? Absolutely not!!

Many people have also tried to use new relationships to avoid dealing with the haunting or traumatic debris or residue, which in fact made it extremely worse because they see or feel that which you've tried to bury. Now, you've hurt or dragged another individual into your mess. Did this help your situation? Absolutely not!!

Some people have dealt with all kinds of abuse prior to getting involved with you. If you have the attitude, perception or view "I don't have time to deal with their insecurities", then you might want to rethink getting involved in any relationship.

People need and are looking for assurance that you're not going to "hurt", betray, lead them on, lie to them, cheat on them, etc. Please take note and understand that there are people that haven't taken time to heal from their wounds. Some folk use other people to try their best to get over folk and in turn hurt them by bringing them into their created foolishness.

This is why those that are abused usually become the abuser without even realizing it. It's important/ imperative to recognize "red flags", signs and inconsistencies in any relationship.

ALWAYS remember that your freedom and your life are equal and are non- negotiable!! - Lamont Bershawn

The problem with avoiding personal healing and development is that it causes a cancerous affect by attacking and attaching itself to deeply embedded situations, which can ultimately end up in a fatal conclusion.

Here it is four years later and I meet a lady named Stephanie, through social media who is an Author of a couple of books. We had a few things in common such as our views towards religion, sports that interested us, traveling and writing. This particular lady lived in a different state, so we would regularly keep in contact. Our conversations were full of laughter, business and futuristic plans. Stephanie started out telling me that she was married three times and had been divorced for five years. Her first husband of twenty-five years has cancer, was physically and psychologically abusive but still living. Her second marriage was an arrangement and her third marriage was extremely abusive in every way possible. Stephanie began telling me that she hadn't seen or heard from her last husband in five years.

I asked Stephanie, "Do you think you're healed from your past marital experiences?" Stephanie replied, "Yes, I'm healed and my name represents the badge of honor. I'm now an advocate for abused women." I asked, "How do you know that you're healed, after all the physical, psychological and emotional abuse that you've endured?" Stephanie responded, "If you could have seen me a few years ago. I was hallucinating, vomiting, malnourished and my hair was falling out. I began building up myself to the point I never looked back." I accepted that response although deep down inside I knew it wasn't an answer. I gave her the benefit of doubt and took a chance of getting to know her. Stephanie never told me her process of becoming a healed woman, she told me what she experienced during that moment and the literal build up {ass injections, boob job and face lift}. The work Stephanie had done to enhance her look only built up her self-esteem, which had nothing to do with her being healed from the abuse.

A few months of daily conversing I flew Stephanie to Reno, Nevada for our initial meeting. We had a blast and really didn't want to depart from each other. The last hour together in Reno I asked her, "How much money did you spend or lose?" Prior to her boarding the airplane I gave her enough money to replenish her bank account.

Please be mindful the reason I gave her the money is I invited her and paid all expenses. I wanted to show her that I'm a true man that takes care of his responsibilities, a man that will never see her without, a man that don't mind giving, a man that will protect, honor and respect her at all times. The problem with spending lots of money so fast and easy is the wrong message is conveyed and one could end up being taken advantage of. Especially, if the individual isn't used to having someone in their lives that was genuine and exemplified true power.

You can rescue, feed and heal a wounded dog but the dog isn't used to being treated well. The dog will bite you (the hand that feeds it) because it doesn't recognize this form of treatment and because you're a total stranger.

You in turn will either kill the dog because if it will bite you once it will more than likely bite you again; or you'll continue to care for the dog based on remembering you decided to rescue the dog from its situation.

What am Eye saying? It's a number of you that hate your relationship, wishing you'd never gotten entangled with that individual or gave them access to your heart.

You're beginning to doubt your decision making based on "falling in love" with a stray. Allow me to give you a little clarity that will help you out in your situation.

The only reason you "fell in love" is because you were in a vulnerable point in your life that was wide open in receiving someone that complimented your state of mind in that particular moment of your life.

Your part is complete! The wounded is healed, they received a balanced diet and now you must move on because you've found out that you're being dragged through the mud and your spirit is being drained.

Keep in mind that hurt people hurt people.

It's impossible to heal someone or from something overnight, especially if they're carrying years of embedded hurt. Just as the wounded dog that you rescued will turn so will some of the people you've helped.

In the end you'll be looked at as the bad person or the person that did something that made them retaliate.

What Eye've learned is that most people love to hear negative things about you because most people are like "crabs in a bucket." The more you achieve or accomplish the more they slander your name.

Don't get upset! Don't worry about getting even!

Wounded people have a way of trying to keep you to themselves. Their intentions are to have the world look at you negatively while they're sprinting back your way, hoping you'll receive them with open arms.

POINT: BE CAREFUL AND MINDFUL OF HELPING FOLK. YOUR HELP ISN'T APPRECIATED AS MUCH AS YOU THINK. EVEN A SNAKE WILL PLAY DEAD IN ORDER TO FILL YOU WITH DEADLY VENOM! – Lamont Bershawn.

Over the next few months, I helped Stephanie through her financial hardships, dealing with her insecurities and in the process, I found out a few of her addictions. I had no idea that she was addicted to prescription drugs and alcohol. Stephanie tried to shield me from finding things out but sooner or later the truth will rise to the surface.

I didn't deny what I saw in her, it just made me embrace Stephanie much tighter because I thought my expression of love would conquer her addiction. You know, deep down inside I was in love with Stephanie and it made me look past her problems because I was naïve to the real issues that she was experiencing. I began ignoring the multiple signs of her mental illness. We kept busy either going to the casino, going shopping, cooking, watching television, writing, flying somewhere, being intimate or me surprising her with gifts.

We made the decision to get married and everything seemed to be getting better between us, so I thought. I had no idea that I had withdrawn myself from noticing her reoccurring triggers. Every once in a while, Stephanie would get quiet and when she began talking again it was as if this little girl was speaking through her. I asked Stephanie, "Are you okay?" Stephanie replied, "Yes. Did I do or say something that gave you a feeling that something was wrong?" I said, "No." It was as if Stephanie was either possessed or in a trance at times because of her actions, the little girls voice and the immediate sexual response after she came to herself.

Stephanie began crying out to me, because she finally was open with me about a few things. I knew about the three ex-husbands mental, emotional and physical abuse. I didn't know about the raping and molestation that took place in her life. I thought to myself, that this is probably why she turns to drugs and alcohol in order to cope with the memory of it all. I felt that if I could give her a change of environment things would change for the better, so I moved her to Pennsylvania with me. Two months into her move with me her entire demeanor changed. Now that I wasn't visiting her, I was able to see her every day and she had to be transparent. The triggers never stopped, the abuse from her was beginning and my tolerance of her living with me was fading away. She was no longer that beautiful lady that I initially met through Facebook she was a demon in disguise.

Stephanie's stepfather died a week later and she took a few days off work to travel and attend the funeral. She was gone six days and called me every day telling me how much she missed me. When I picked her up from the airport, she hugged me as if she never wanted to let me go. I didn't allow that to change my view about what I was actually experiencing with her.

The following week we were off to Las Vegas. I never cancelled the planned trip that would have taken place after our wedding and I still allowed Stephanie to go although things between us were becoming sour. When we arrived in Vegas, I realized the only time she enjoyed with me was when we were at the casinos gambling. I knew that Stephanie knew that things changed between us because I wasn't so willing to freely give her any longer. This is when Stephanie's true colors came to the surface. She cussed me out in public because I didn't allow her to borrow any money, after I gave her five hundred dollars as soon as we got situated in the hotel for whatever she wanted to use it for. My perception of Stephanie was that she was ungrateful, misguided and heavily addicted to drugs. My spirit wouldn't allow me to become intimate with her that entire week in Las Vegas because she didn't act like herself, didn't look like herself and I was no longer connected to this individual.

Please understand that your spirit is ALWAYS in protective mode. This is why it's important and IMPERATIVE to be in tune with your consciousness. The moment you question yourself or your action to allow your flesh or belief to give an answer, you'll realize that evil is always present in your space or circle. It's waiting the opportune time to devour you. This is why you must beware of the decoy that will distract you in order to set you up for destruction.

S/N: A "distraction" will be a disruptive disturbance that takes your focus away from anything important. This is why some of you have become sidetracked and it has caused years of delay with your promise.

The essence of who you are will NEVER disconnect from the source. You're powerful beyond what anyone can see. Remember, the "enemy" gains your power by connecting to the "inner me" and drains your "energy" by intoxicating your "inner-G!" - Lamont Bershawn

I couldn't wait to get back home because it was necessary for me to hurry up and get Stephanie out of my home and my presence because I knew that my freedom was in jeopardy. I realized that Stephanie was telling a few lies about her previous relationships and marriages. In my eyes Stephanie was a manic depressive, bipolar and schizophrenic. I found out that my brother, Jerome reached out to her and put a lot of negative thoughts in her head that she believed and he ended up having sex with her. Why would my own brother want to violate the "brotherly code?" It's because he saw me as his opponent and not his brother.

HEY YOU!! YES, YOU!!

Don't get upset when someone looks at you as their competition.

They're only setting the bar higher for themselves because your walk, your path, your lifestyle, your ambition and your knowledge/wisdom has vexed their lives.

They're wondering why so much "good" is happening to you. Why so many doors have opened in your favor?

It's not because you prayed, fasted or paid tithes to any religious organization. It's not because you made a deal with the "devil." It's not because you have so many initials behind your name. It's not because you've kissed so much ass until you smell shit for days and it's not because you "sexed" your way to the top.

So many doors have opened in your favor because you've recognized your true purpose which in turn will keep you "productively progressing."

Many of you have allowed your gifts and skill to lay dormant while you search for ways to achieve your personal goals.

It reminds me of bowling. Each person must approach the line and throw the bowl for themselves. You can still throw a perfect game, (300) and the team can still lose. Once you understand this concept, you'll see your greatest competitor!! –Lamont Bershawn.

YOUR greatest competitor is YOURSELF!!

When Stephanie departed my home for the last time, she called me two days later asking me if she could borrow two-hundred dollars. I told Stephanie that I think it would be best for her to move on without using me as one of her crutches. I hung up the phone and closed the chapter.

Later that evening, I decided to take my mother to dinner at the casino. I just wanted to get out of the house and get some air because I truly dodged a missile knowing what I now know to be true about Stephanie. While we were sitting at the table my mother said, "I don't get involved with your business or your relationships, but I knew that she wasn't the one for you." I asked her, "How did you know?" My mother replied, "She was too needy for one. She thought you had a gold mine somewhere because you were able to bail her out of her situations. She fell more for your ability to give to her opposed to your heart. Secondly, she carried too much mental and emotional baggage. I knew you loved her unconditionally and wanted things to work, so I didn't say anything."

"Don't ever put yourself in a situation to become broke for an individual. A person enters your life to enhance what's already there.

It's okay to wine and dine an individual, but don't get sidetracked creating a lifestyle for them that they didn't desire for themselves.

You'll find yourself being drained while they're using you as a stepping stone or step ladder." – Lamont Bershawn.

Mom wanted to gamble a little after we ate. She went to play her machine and I walked around to my Buffalo machine. There was an empty seat next to a beautiful young lady, so I asked her, "Is anyone playing here?" She replied, "Not unless you see someone that I don't", as she smiled. I sat down and began playing the slot machine and she began winning. She looked over at me and said, "You should have sat next to me a longtime ago." I told her, "I had no intention on coming to the casino, but I brought my mother here to eat, but I'm glad that I did because I'm sitting here next to you." What's your name? She said, "Butterfly." Well hello, "Butterfly" my name is Lamont. "Hello Lamont", she replied. We sat next to each other for a few hours laughing, joking around, picking the bonus for each other and making fun wagers. It was as if the Universe or God wanted me to realize that genuine love was still available for me. Butterfly and I exchanged telephone numbers. If anyone would have walked by, they would have thought that we were either a couple or thought that we knew each other. That's how strong our connection was in such a short period of time.

Relationship 146:

It's up to you to recognize if you're involved with a "BUILDER" or a "BURDEN."

A "BUILDER" will help increase or enhance your value.

A "BURDEN" will decrease or destroy everything from your potential to your progress. - Lamont Bershawn

    I was having so much fun and I realized that I needed to go check on my mother. When I called my mother her voicemail picked up, but then I remembered that she rarely brings her phone inside the casino. I asked Butterfly to hold my seat for a few minutes. She said ok. I walked around for a few minutes until I saw my mother sitting there as the slot attendant was paying her. When I got up closer, I realized my mother won over three thousand dollars on the slot machine. My mother looked up and smiled at me. I asked her, "Do you want me to hold any of it and deposit it into your account when we leave?" Mom gave me twenty- five hundred dollars to hold in order for it to be deposited into the credit union. I walked back over and sat next to Butterfly. Butterfly asked, "How's mom doing?" I said, "Well, she just hit a hand pay that was over three thousand dollars playing the other Buffalo game." Within a matter of ten minutes Butterfly hit a hand pay and ten minutes after that I hit a hand pay. Needless to say, it was an amazing night. Here it is almost midnight and I had to get up for work in the morning, so mom came over and I introduced Butterfly to my mother. While my mother used the restroom, I walked Butterfly to her car, kissed and hugged her and we both said, "It was an honor to meet you."

    Butterfly made me feel special in a short period of time. I believe it was an introduction of purpose and a meeting of peace designed to let me know that the desires of my heart could be met if I began looking internally instead accepting the external quality of an individual.

My mother said, "Butterfly is classy, have great mannerism, qualities that makes her stand out and she's someone that she could see me marrying." Butterfly is an Aquarius like me and we have so much in common. To some a butterfly is a symbol of peace, but to me it's a symbol of strength because a caterpillar must die unto itself in order to become a butterfly. In other words, a caterpillar must hang upside down in a cocoon {its own casket} and must be resurrected in order to fly.

The following weekend my mother was on her way out of town to attend her churches convention and I gathered everything Stephanie left at my house. I put everything inside of a black trash bag and set it on fire, burning every spirit that was attached to her belongings. I wasn't sure if Stephanie tried working roots or witchcraft against me but I wasn't taking any chances. I immediately did a spiritual cleanse and detox to rid any residue of her from my being.

Have you DETOXED lately?

I guess many are asking, "What's the purpose of this question?"

Allow me to answer it like this:

Often times we go through the hustle and bustle of life dealing with so much junk that it's caused us to be intoxicated. Yes, our bodies have an internal filtration system, but that even gets clogged at some point.

A Psychological, Physical and Spiritual DETOX is necessary, essential and IMPERATIVE for life's existence!!

A Psychological Detox is necessary to rid your minds of ALL of the junk/ mess that you've been carrying for a period of time. This deals

with {but NOT limited to} (1) Negative seeds planted mentally from your childhood (2) being rejected

(3) Being called out of your name {bitch, nigger, faggot, whore, fat, etc.} that you've openly accepted (4) you'll never mount to be anything (5) seeing someone murdered (6) seeing a tragic accident (6) UNFORGIVING, etc.

A *Physical Detox* is necessary to rid your body {internally/ externally} of the intoxicants that are causing problems. This deals with {but NOT limited to}

(1) Skin disease (2) Different types of Cancers (3) SEXUAL PARTNERS {women: those men that you've allowed to cum/ ejaculate inside of you without protection that's causing you to have a horrible odor. You're probably having a discharge that isn't from a yeast infection, so get it checked out. Men: those women that you've had unprotected anal sex with as well as those women who you've had unprotected vaginal sex with and have NOT properly cleansed {circumcised or uncircumcised}, it's time to do so. Nonoxynol-9 {lubricant found in condoms} is a detergent that harms the cell walls of the vagina, causes irritation and chronic infection and doubles the risk of STI infection. I know you're damned if you do and damned if you don't, but this is REAL TALK!! (4) Have you ever met someone with halitosis {stink breath}? Part of the problem is they don't take a shit on a regular basis, so their system becomes backed up. The problem is from holding waste within. "WHAT GOES IN MUST COME OUT!!"

A *Spiritual Detox* is necessary to rid your being of religious doctrine, dogmas, principles, disciplines and beliefs that makes a person deny their AUTHENTIC connection to God. It's very IMPORTANT to COMMUNE with SELF in order to see yourself/ GET TO KNOW YOURSELF from your own perspective instead of viewing yourself out of the eyes of someone else. This deals with {but NOT limited to}

(1) Religious organizations/ Institutions that distort or imprison the minds of the people (2) Scare Tactics used to make people live in fear

(3) Apotropaic Rituals to ward off evil {Sometimes the "ENEMY" you're trying to escape is the "In- Um- E" in ME {Self}.

Once you've had a COMPLETE DETOXIFICATION, I assure you that you'll be able to (1) THINK clearly and with LOGIC (2) Feel better about SELF (3) Look better to SELF/ OTHERS (4) LIVE an abundant and happier life. - Lamont Bershawn.

Was the process of removing someone you were in love with and invested in easy? Absolutely not! I admit the first couple of nights were hard because I had night sweats and the shakes. Yep, I was like "Pookie" from the movie, "New Jack City" when he was kicking his drug addiction. I realized that my flesh and spirit was deeper into Stephanie than I thought. I was really in love with her and had expectations of marrying her, but the process of getting set free was necessary. Two weeks after the spiritual cleanse and detox I was back to myself. I'm now focused on my upcoming projects, book promotions and writing more material.

A few days later I receive a phone call from Butterfly asking me, "Would you like to go to the Tracey Morgan Show? He's performing at the casino." I replied, "Sure." I met Butterfly at the front door and she was extremely stunning. We greeted each other, grabbed a few snacks and entered into the stadium. When we got our seats, we held hands and was enjoying the moment. Tracey Morgan's performance was funny and amazing to say the least. After the show we grabbed a bite to eat and spent a few intimate hours together listening to music and engaging in an awesome dialogue. I gave Butterfly a gift, along with a personal poem that I had written for her and we kissed and parted ways. Little did I know, but this would be the last time I saw Butterfly because she moved further away.

20/20 which is considered "normal vision" because both eyes can see a group of letters good at a distance of 20 feet.

Often times, our vision become impaired through the "lens" of social media, life experience, personal hurt, relationships, our personal choices/ decisions and other people's view/ perception that have been planted in our minds.

Over the years, most of you either have listened to the negativity from others about you or have been struggling with negative seeds that have been planted and have grown within you until you've totally lost hope or the ability to define yourself. In other words, you've taken a stranger's belief about you as being actual and factual.

Allow me to encourage a few people this morning:

This is your year for renewed vision because your success will be based off how you visualize or view things that you're involved with.

You've entered this year with a new vision, a renewed mindset, a new perspective of life, a new objective and a different standing point.

S/N: DON'T BE DISCOURAGED IF SOMEONE CONSIDERS YOU TO BE ABNORMAL!!

While "regular" folk are sound asleep you being the visionary is still awake making your vision come alive. You see, you have got to get to the point that people aren't just calling you abnormal, but crazy!!

Your 2020 will be abundant, enhanced and prosperous!!

REALITY: Don't get perplexed, sidetracked, bent out of shape or even upset when you find out that your significant other was one of your greatest hindrances. As you were planning and planting, they were scheming and demeaning.

This is your year to see things more clearly.

In other words, you'll know who has your best interest at heart beyond words and actions. You'll be able to differentiate between those real friends and fake folk!!

My first question in 2020 for YOU is, "Can you see clearly now?"

– Lamont Bershawn.

Here I am single and free once again giving myself time to reflect and heal from my previous relationship. I knew what her wrongdoings were but it was time for me as a man to acknowledge what I did wrong during the relationship. I realized that I did so much to financially prove myself that I was capable of supporting her and picking her up in order to prevent her from falling. I also tried to "love all of her hurt and insecurities away." The truth of the matter is no one has the ability to heal other individuals hurt or pain away because that's their personal experience. I also went wrong with allowing myself to become emotional when she attacked me. Why? It's because men naturally are warriors and the need to protect is innate. Men stand their ground because psychologically it becomes a sign of weakness to bow out or not verbally respond. It's also because there was something within me or my spirit that I thought I had gotten over, but that area of my still had a scab on it and I realized that I still needed to be healed. People that have experienced being a victim of all forms of abuse will absorb every encounter and will eventually become an abuser if they refused to be healed. The first part of being healed is admitting or confessing to yourself that you have a problem. The next step is to withdraw from the situation. It's impossible to remain connected to the abuser or the victim during your healing process. When a person gets mad, they usually get mad because they have no control. If they have no control then the "inner-me" finds a way to cause the lower vibration of an individual to surface in order to bring their lower self-esteem into action. Now the control factor is present and the degradation, devaluing and disrespect come into play because they have now created an atmosphere where they mentally have the upper hand.

Don't ever underestimate the power of suggestion or persuasion.

The power of "suggestion" and "persuasion" are very similar and very simple as it will take you off your personal path or course to follow that of another individual. It's very dangerous as it will cause you:

1) Years of delay

2) To be in the shadow of another

3) To block or devalue your own worth because you've lost yourself trying to be someone you weren't created to be

4) To deny your natural sense or abilities

5) To believe something is real when in fact it's a façade

6) To get you lost in the "sauce" in order to make you forget you're a "boss."

To persuade someone simply means to believe something, especially after a sustained effort. To convince people, Pastors/ Preachers attempt to persuade their congregants by appealing to their emotions using humor, instilling fear and using scare tactics.

Examples:

1) If you don't do this or that you will not be blessed

2) God can't use you if you're...

3) You're going to Hell if you...

ALL of this is said to PERSUADE {the congregation} to do what they'd like for you to do. This is NOT limited to religious be-LIE-fs or organizations!!

To "suggest" simply means to cause one to think that (something) exists or is the case.

The power of "suggestion" is based on the psychological mechanism that whatever the subconscious accepts, it acts on.

Examples:

1) I hope I can get at least three people to shout.

2) You should date/ marry that individual because you both have a lot in common

There are many other examples of the power of suggestion including implication, distraction, association, or metaphor.

POINT: You have to be careful of the information that you entertain; because with it comes the spirit that endorse it. If you're NOT strong enough to handle the spirit that endorse it, you can end up being confused trying to find the truth in an atmosphere of falsehood. It's IMPOSSIBLE to find TRUTH when the FOUNDATION of it is a LIE!!! - Lamont Bershawn.

Two years pass by and now it's time for my second book, "Eye've Stood Inside the Eye of Hell and Remained Fearless" to be promoted and released. This book goes deeper into knowing yourself and recognizing the power within instead of conforming to other people's perception of you.

It doesn't matter what state you were born in whether it was the great states of Pennsylvania, N. Carolina, Texas or New Jersey; we were ALL born in the state of "messed up."

When a person desires to compete against you it's because they're intimated by you and really wish they could be "like" you. They've psychologically created a "race" and you're being challenged; the only thing is that you don't know it.

S/N: This DOESN'T EXCLUDE your spouse, significant other, sibling, friend or parent's!! Just because they're close DON'T mean they want the best thing for you out of life's journey!!

It's when that individual feels they're losing the "race" all hell breaks loose because they begin attacking your character and your lifestyle in order to make others view you negatively.

Why? It's because people "naturally" believe or gravitate to negative things or lies concerning others because it makes them feel superior.

This is why it's imperative to understand the three: "I", "Eye" and "Aye!"

"I" represents the path of an individual when they're possessed in learning who they are.

"Eye" represents understanding and having knowledge of my path. In other words, Eye recognize my purpose, my walk, my power and Eye consciously see what's going on around me.

"Aye" represents a deeper value of the "inner-G" of the

"Inner-ME." My solid stance of "M.E." {Metaphysically Evolving}!!

- Lamont Bershawn.

I felt better about the release of this book because I had a different publisher and more people could better understand my perception of things. Here it is doors are beginning to open more, people are asking me to join their podcast for interviews and people are beginning to message me letting me know how my words have encouraged them. I must be honest and say that since I left the church I've felt so much at peace and free. I recall receiving a message from one of my former colleagues in the ministry asking me, "Do you think you still have the gift of gab?"

I responded, "Absolutely! It's not hard to create a power packed, emotional story that people would be drawn to."

What some may consider a "gift" really isn't one it's just a way to "manipulate" the craft of being in something for a long time.

Eye can go to anyone's church, sit in anyone's pulpit and still mesmerize the people using the name of "Jesus" like the Pied Piper.

When people are so hurt, so lost, so disgusted, so upset or angry and feel the need to hear from "Jesus"; it doesn't take long for them to adhere because it's the name they're attached to.

Eye say attached and not connected for the fact when an individual becomes awakened THAT name becomes obsolete.

When Eye was in church Eye knew it was all about the presentation of the story to make them feel it {like this} ...

There was a young man who had a wife and two children. He was laid off and his bank account was in the negative. His wife was unemployed and the only income was his. He didn't want to tell his wife because he didn't want her to worry or look at him as a failure.

The next morning, he left the house as if nothing changed but he didn't go to work. His first stop was "Job Corps." Job Corps told him they had nothing for him.

His second stop was back at the previous job to speak with the "EEOC" {Equal Employment Opportunity Commission} but they told him there's nothing they could do.

Leaving no stone "un-turned" he visits the "Salvation Army." They send him away with a few used threads.

He leaves there and heads to the "Unemployment office." The clerk tells him that he's overqualified for anything in their system.

The young man is so distraught that he goes to the "SSA" {Social Security Administration}. When his number gets called, he approaches the desk. The lady tells him he's too young to collect social security.

He finally gets back home and loads his .44 Magnum. He writes his wife a farewell letter ending with "I loved you all." As he places the barrel of the pistol in his mouth while tears are flowing from his eyes, he cocks the hammer back and an Angel appears.

The Angel calls him by name and says, "Take the gun out of your mouth and lay it on the table, God heard your cry and felt your silent tears." As a matter of fact, "HE" guided your every step so that you'd never forget. Go backtrack or revisit your travels today!! {Angel disappears}.

The young man unloads his pistol, rips up the letter and becomes excited about seeing his family.

P.S. It's all in the message!!
J- Job Corps
E- Equal Employment Opportunity Commission
S- Salvation Army
U- Unemployment Office
S- Social Security Administration

Eye'm sure some of you all are probably crying and shouting now!!

The answers to your situations, problems and circumstances are within as well as the power to change them!! - Lamont Bershawn.

Things are going extremely well for me at this point in my life. I've healed from my previous relationship, my relationship with family seemed to be back on track and my finances are gaining a boost. I'm in a position in my life that I'm able to freely breathe and travel promoting my book. It's now October and I'm looking to purchase a truck for deer hunting because I didn't want to drive my car in the mountains just in case it was snowing. I take a moment to browse Facebook and I see a friend post and as I go read a few comments I see a photo of a young lady that resembles Melissa, the young lady I previously spoke about. When I clicked on her picture and saw her smile on her profile, I knew it was her. I became excited because the young lady that I've searched for was finally able to be reached. I sent her a message in hopes that she'd respond, but no response. I sent her a friend request and it lingered for a week without being accepted. Melissa finally accepted my request and I immediately sent her another message and commented on her photo. Melissa responds, "Is it okay that I message you?" I replied, "Absolutely." I didn't hesitate to ask, "Do you remember me?" Melissa replied, "No, I can't say that I do. All I know is that you're very handsome." "Thank you", I responded. "Please forgive me but I don't mean to disrespect your wife or relationship", Melissa replied. I immediately sent her my number and asked Melissa to call me. Melissa replied, "I don't call married men. My daddy told me to never call married or involved men." I quickly responded, "I'm single." Melissa sent me her number and I didn't hesitate to call. When I called Melissa and she answered the phone I must say that I was extremely happy just to know that she was alive. I asked her again, "You mean to tell me that you forgot all about me?" Melissa asked, "Where would I remember you from?" I walked Melissa through memory lane just to see if I could say something that would jar a portion of her memory. I asked her, "Do you remember making love with me?" Melissa said, "Now, I know you have the wrong person because I never forget my partners." Melissa paused for a moment and asked, "Do you have a light skinned grandmother?" I said, "Yes." "Are you from Pennsylvania?" I said, "Yes." Melissa became so excited and began hyperventilating saying, "I know, I know, I know who you are!" I replied, "Who am I?" Melissa said, "You're my first love." I was so glad she remembered me. As the conversation progressed Melissa told me that she was married three times and was single. She took it upon herself to raise her third husband's two children who were at the ages of thirteen and fifteen. She told me that her biological child was in the military and married, but was on the outs with his wife and lived with her. I asked Melissa, "Where are you living now?" She told me that she was currently in Georgia and had been there a few months. She also told me that she was a Registered Nurse on the military base where her son was stationed. Melissa asked, "What happened to you? I thought you were coming back to get me?" I said, "When I came back, I looked for you at the trailer and it was boarded up. I asked a few people that I knew and they had no clue and I called the number you gave me and the number was disconnected. So, what happened to you?" Melissa responded, "I was pregnant and my father put me out of the house. He told me that I had one child already that they were helping me take care of and it would be best that I got rid of it. My mother took me to the abortion clinic and when everything was all over, I became rebellious, moved to another state and got married." "Melissa, I received one letter from you and I responded immediately and you never shared this with me", I replied.

What are you doing next weekend Melissa? I'll be in North Carolina and I'd love to see you if you're available. "I don't have any plans and I'd love to see you in person after being away from you for twenty-six years", Melissa responded. Okay Melissa, I have to get some rest because I have to get up at 5:00 a.m. for work. Rest well and I'll see you on Friday. The next morning, I texted Melissa and told her to have an amazing day and Melissa responded with a morning call. We talked briefly and she asked if she could borrow a few dollars for gas money. I asked her for her cash app name and sent her forty dollars. Later that evening when I got off work, I called Melissa while I was on my way home. We talked in depth about a few things and she was very apologetic for not waiting for my return. Once I explained to her that everything happens for a reason in due season and the past can't be undone, she said, "As long as I have you back in my life, I'm good." Finally, it's Friday morning and I'm at work counting down the hours before I hit the road. Melissa calls me and asks if I can cash app her sixty dollars to travel with? Melissa tells me that she needs to get her hair and nails done too because she didn't want to look raggedy our first meeting after being away for so long. I sent her the money she needed and asked her to call me when she hit the road. When I got off work and went home, I showered and was ready to hit the road. I called Melissa to see if she was packed, but she was still getting her hair done and I overheard the hairstylist say, "Ask him for the money to pay me?" Melissa asked me and I immediately asked her, "What did you do with the money I sent you?" Melissa said, "I got my hair done." I told Melissa, "You're starting things off wrong by doing the absolute opposite of what you said you needed the money for." Melissa said, "You're right. I apologize but I didn't want to come see you without having my hair done. As soon as she's done, we're going to hit the road. My check will be deposited into my account in a couple of days, so can you cash app me another sixty and I'll give it back to you in a few days?" I ended up sending her the money for traveling. We ended up meeting at the Circle K gas station off exit forty-nine in North Carolina, after she dropped her children off at her mother's house. I ended up hopping in the car with her and driving her vehicle to the house because she was tired. When we arrived at the house, I grabbed all of the bags from both vehicles and I was finally able to relax a little. We looked at each other and hugged each other as if it were a lifetime being away from each other. I mean it has been twenty-six years and so much in both of our lives changed. I took a shower and then she took a shower and once we got settled in, I gave her a bottle of perfume along with a card. When she read the card, her eyes became full of tears. I asked, "Why are you crying?" Melissa said, "I've been longing to feel these words being manifested for so long. I know these words to be true because it's similar to what you've said to me in a letter approximately twenty-five years ago." She sprayed a little of the perfume on and loved it. We lay down next to one another in the bed and began cuddling as she lay in my arms with her head on my chest. I kissed Melissa on the forehead and said, "I've been waiting for this moment for twenty-six years since the first time we met and made love." Melissa leaned up and kissed me on my lips and then proceeded to lick around the circumference of my mouth with her tongue, until she slipped her tongue into my mouth touching my tongue. Melissa said, "I've never stopped thinking about you and often wondered what I'd feel when and if we were to ever see each other again." I asked, "What do you feel?" Melissa said, "Like this!" Melissa began disrobing me and kissing me on my neck. She then straddled me as she began licking, biting and sucking my nipples. She got a little lower and put her tongue in the seat of my navel while she looked up into my eyes and said, "I never felt free enough to do this with any other man." I began thinking, "Stop lying! You're trying to manipulate me and psychologically pull me into your world. My thought was very different than the verbal response which was, "You've been married three times and never felt this free, then why me?" Melissa started sucking my dick and said, "You were my first love and actually the only man that I've ever truly loved." I didn't respond to her as I flipped her over and began undressing her. I whispered into the canal of her ear and the message traveled to her thalamus, which sent vibrations to her clitoris. It was similar to that of a "Welcome address" and the "Intense Response" of a gladiator in battle after the sound of the trumpet. The passion was intense, the atmosphere was perfect and our attachment was still powerful.

Eye'm not sure who needs to read this but you're in a "questionable" relationship.

Your relationship is on a rollercoaster ride, a seesaw or in a canoe without a paddle.

You two hit it off from the moment you laid eyes on each other and had a few conversations.

Allow me to give you a little relief --------------> IT'S NOT YOU!!

The problem is that you have a stronger connection to the potential that you see in the individual than the individual themselves.

NOTE: NOT EVERYONE WILL REACH THE POTENTIAL THAT YOU SEE IN THEM!!

Some folk are comfortable in their situation, circumstance or dilemma and don't want anything better out of life, but would rather bring you into their mess.

FACT: "SUCCESS IS A MENTALITY THAT MOST PEOPLE HAVE TURNED INTO A LIFESTYLE!!"

There's a lot of rich folk that die broke!!

You've become attached to the potential and connected to the lie.

Please understand there's a difference between being attached to something/ someone opposed to being connected.

Being attached does NOT mean there's a connection.

An attachment consists of something/ someone that's DEPENDENT upon the other.

Example:

(1) {A leech/ parasite feeding off a living organism for survival}

(2) {One sided relationship}

(3) {A hook and cable towing a car}

A connection is a collective, equal partisan, dual shared union/ meeting on common ground. Two individual parallels coming together forming one powerful unit.

Example:

(1) {An electrical light switch}

(2) {Two people coming together creating an intimate port}

(3) {Causal or logical relation or sequence}

Some of you are in a relationship and you're:

(1) Wondering why you're still there...

(2) Wondering why things aren't working out ...

(3) Wondering why you're not getting the attention that you feel you deserve...

(4) Wondering who the hell is this person... because it's certainly NOT the individual you gave access to your heart.

Well, have you ever thought or considered that you're ONLY attached to the person and there's no REAL CONNECTION?

POINT: Recognizing your connection is more valuable than misunderstanding/ misinterpreting your attachment to anything/ anyone!!- Lamont Bershawn.

The next morning, Melissa went to her parent's house to check on her children and to handle business with her mother. My mother was scheduled to look at a few homes since she was in the market of selling and relocating. Since Melissa went to handle business, I went with my mother so that she wouldn't be taken advantage of and also because I wanted to make sure she was getting her money's worth without the scams behind real estate. Later that evening Melissa returned with her children so they could be introduced to me. Her youngest child needed a haircut so I offered to cut his hair in order to save her a few dollars. Melissa's oldest son told me that the car's radiator was leaking and began overheating. When I looked at the car, I realized that the leak was coming from a broken neck on the radiator. I went to the auto parts store and purchased a tee for the hose and gorilla glue in order to splice the hose and make a connector. Melissa also called her sister Sandra to come over to meet me after she left her job. When Sandra came over, I walked over to her and introduced myself.

Sandra looked at me and said, "I don't remember you but I've heard so many troubling things concerning your brother Jerome." I looked at Sandra and said, "I'm not sure what you heard but I'm nothing like him." I walked away and sat on the porch to allow Melissa to spend a few moments with her sister. When Sandra left Melissa walked over to me and said, "Jerome has a bad wrap around town and it's a great thing that you're only visiting because people will make the mistake of thinking you're just like your brother." I explained a little about me and Jerome's relationship to Melissa. Funny thing is Melissa said that she felt his conflicting energy when she saw him. I knew it was getting late and Melissa had to soon leave to head back to Georgia but I wanted to make sure the car was in good driving condition or at least would make it back to her destination. I called a few times to make sure the car wasn't overheating and to make sure they had enough money for food and gas. I made it back to Pennsylvania an hour before she made it to Georgia. When I got settled and ready for bed, I waited for Melissa to call before I went to sleep just to make sure she made it home safely. Melissa called me when she made it home and got things settled. Melissa said, "It was great spending time with you and I hope we can see each other again real soon." I replied, "I'd love to spend more quality time with you."

The next morning, when I arrived at work, I called Melissa to make sure everything was okay. Melissa answered the phone and told me that her electric was turned off. She said, "I get paid on Tuesday so I'll wait." I responded, "Why would you wait until tomorrow when everything in your place runs off electricity including your stove?" Melissa said, "You've done enough for me and I don't want you to think that I'm taking advantage of you? If you're able to pay the bill for me, I'll be sure to cash app you your money as soon as I get paid." I asked Melissa, "How much is your electric bill?" Melissa replied, "My bill is $165.00." "Okay, call them on three-way and enter your information so that I can use my credit card to pay your bill." Melissa thanked me and said, "I really appreciate all that you're doing for me." "It's no problem. I couldn't allow you all to be left out in the cold or the dark. Allow me to get to work and I'll call you when I get off. Have a great day", I responded. When I hung up the phone with Melissa something wasn't sitting right with my spirit and I knew I had to have a heart to heart conversation with her. When I got home and settled, I called Melissa and asked her, "Are you busy or are you available to talk?" Melissa said, "I'm free to talk." Allow me to start this conversation off with saying, "I totally understand that people struggle through life, get caught up in bad situations and sometimes don't know how to get out of the rut but are you currently working?" Melissa responded, "No. I'm a registered nurse. I was working on base and had to leave." "Why did you leave your job?" Melissa answered, "My husband almost killed me and it was best for me to immediately leave for the sake of my life and my children." I replied, "I'm so sorry that you had to go through that." Melissa, it's amazing how life deals us cards according to the decisions we make. I would have never thought in one million years that my life would have taken the course that it did, but I made it through. "What are you doing the day after Thanksgiving Day?" Melissa said, "I don't have any plans, why?" "How would you like to go deer hunting with me?" Melissa replied, "I'd love to go hunting with you." "Okay, let me look online for flights so I can purchase your airline ticket", I replied. Melissa said, "Is it possible that you can send me a few dollars for gas?" "Sure." Melissa said, "I wish I could take the children to the fair tonight; rides are free tonight. "How much is the fee to enter the fair?" "The cost is three dollars per person tonight", Melissa replied. I cash app Melissa money for gas and money to take the children to the fair. Later that same evening when Melissa video called me, I asked her, "How was the fair?" Melissa said, "We didn't go because I had to buy a few groceries to put food on the table. In my heart I felt that Melissa was trying to swindle me, she was bad with her finances or she was lying to me all around because it was easy for me to send her money whenever she asked for it. A couple of weeks went by and Melissa had a disagreement with her oldest son, Paul. Melissa volunteered to share information about her son's life to me saying, "Paul is a married man and should be living with his wife. That's why he got kicked out of the military for doing things he had no business doing and lying to the military police." I told Melissa, "That really wasn't fair to share his personal information with me without his approval. Please hang the phone up with me and get things in order with your son because he's the one that cares for your children when you're not there. You have to understand that the both of you need each other because in reality you're all that you have." Melissa hung up the phone and called me back a couple of hours later. When Melissa called me back, she said, "Thank you for being transparent enough to tell me that I was wrong. Paul would like to speak with you if that's okay with you?" "Absolutely", I replied. "Hello Lamont. Hello Paul, what is it that you'd like to speak with me about?" Paul said, "I just wanted to thank you for telling my mother that she was wrong. My mother apologized to me and said it was because of what you said to her." "Paul, I know it's hard for you to be a man and want to achieve so many things with a black cloud hanging over your head. I don't know your situation but I felt if I was to hear it, it should be coming from you." Paul said, "Well, I got kicked out of the military and have to go to court to see if what they're going to do about my release. The military wants to give me a discharge of other than honorable. The military police said that I was driving a car under the influence and accidentally hit an officer with the car and never stopped. It was three people in the car and I wasn't driving." "Did you know the other people in the car?" Paul replied, "I knew the girl but didn't know the guy." The story sounded a little fishy to me as I knew he was holding back details, so I gave him an attorney's office to contact. I knew Melissa needed a babysitter to watch the children when she flew up to come hunting with me so it was important that she made everything right with her son. He needed a few dollars because he wasn't employed and Melissa needed someone she could trust and depend on to take the children to school, pick them up from school and feed them.

    A week prior to Melissa flying up for the hunting trip, she received a call from two nursing facilities. Melissa called me one afternoon while I was at work saying, "I have to take an online pretest for my job, I also have to pay for some other form of screening and I need gas to get there." I told her congratulations and didn't hesitate sending her the money she needed. Melissa got the job and told me that she'd be working as a registered nurse at the nursing home passing out meds to the patients. The day before Melissa was supposed to catch her flight, she called me and told me that Paul wanted three hundred dollars to take care of the children for the entire week. Melissa and I agreed to pay half each, but I'd send the entire balance and Melissa would pay her half to me. The next evening when Melissa landed, I picked her up from the airport and we went to grab a bite to eat. When we arrived to the house, I pulled out the hunting gear for her to try on so I could see if I needed to purchase anything. The hunting gear fit perfectly so she began getting her other belongings situated and we went to bed.

The next morning, I had to get up for work and didn't realize I had been on my job for one year, so my Supervisor came by to give me an evaluation. Once I received my evaluation my Supervisor gave me a few company gear cards to purchase work gear and a nice financial raise. Later that evening, my dad stopped by and dropped off Jerome's hunting license into the mail slot since we really weren't speaking because of the foul shit he did to my mother.

"It's a son's duty to always look out for his mother, even when her husband doesn't." - Lamont Bershawn.

Jerome is a convicted felon so he really wasn't supposed to be going hunting, but because my Uncle's health wasn't that great and probably would be his last time ever hunting, I decided to take the license with me to give to Jerome. Did I trust Jerome? Absolutely not! This is why whenever we've gone hunting Jerome hunts in a totally different area than me. Melissa and I rested up and left the house around midnight after making sure we had everything we needed packed inside of the vehicle. Jerome called me earlier to see if I packed his license and to see what time we would be leaving so that we could meet around the same time. We met in McDonald's parking lot in Clearfield County, PA. I gave him his hunting license to sign. Jerome was accompanied by Jill, the young lady he introduced us to in North Carolina that was from Alabama. We began putting on our hunting gear so that we could head towards the hunting area parking lot. We saw a few deer walking on the side of the mountain which seemed to be a good sign that we'd see a few in the woods. When we got into the woods, I spotted Melissa near me and she fell asleep after about an hour. It's usually a little snow on the ground so that spotting a deer is a little easier but this time we had to deal with the blended land. When Melissa awakened a few hours later we saw Jerome and Jill walking on the road near us. Melissa walked to the parking area with Jill and Jerome while I stayed in the hunting spot a little longer. Nothing crossed my path so I decided to make my way to the vehicle to get a bite to eat. When I arrived at the truck Melissa was sitting in the passenger seat with the truck running listening to music. Melissa said, "Did you see anything at all? You were out there a long time." I said, "No. I didn't see anything. It's not a lot of hunters out here this year but hopefully we get an opportunity to take some meat home. In the event that we don't see anything at all it was just a pleasure having you along with me on the trip." When Melissa and I left out of the woods we went to the hotel to check in and went to the Chinese restaurant to get a bite to eat. We left there and stopped by Walmart to pick up a few things and went back to the room to get situated for the next morning. Melissa called to check on her children and to see if they needed anything. Paul told her that everything was perfectly fine, not to worry just enjoy herself. Melissa told Paul thank you and held the phone. Paul thought she hung up the phone and he began talking to his stepdad's daughter telling her, "He used to be the finest bitch in the club." Melissa said, "Paul, what did you just say?" Paul responded {shamefully}, "You heard me?" Melissa said, "Yes." "Paul said, "Goodnight" as he immediately got off the phone. Melissa seemed shock as to what she heard her son say but when I asked her, "Did she know that her son was homosexual?" Melissa said, "I've known for years and just refused to accept it." I looked at Melissa and said, "I know that you've been deeply rooted in the church, but continue to love your son despite what the church says. Your son isn't an abomination nor is he a disappointment to you." Melissa began opening up more to me about her marriage and she was only telling me about her husband's indiscretions without revealing her very own. She also opened up about her maternal grandfather who was a preacher that molested her at a young age. I asked Melissa, "How many times have you been molested and or raped?" Melissa began saying, "Too many times to name and all by people that I trusted." I asked her, "Have you ever sought counseling?" Melissa responded, "My mother is a therapist and she counsels me." At that moment it was important for me to let her know that the individual who helped sway your mind away from your reality could never properly counsel you. This is probably why your mother sticks deep inside the church because she wants God to believe that she's sorry for neglecting to protect you and also why she spends so much on material items for you. It's an expression to make you feel good and something done to remove her guilt.

The next morning, we went back into the woods early and on the way, we saw a few doe cross in front of the vehicle which seemed to be another good sign that we'd see something while hunting. We hunted a few hours and still didn't see anything. We headed back to the hotel early and watched the football game. I'm not sure if Jerome had enough money for another night but he and Jill ended up staying with us that night and slept in the other bed. The next morning, Jerome and Jill packed their vehicle and headed back home while Melissa and I went back to the woods for the last day of hunting. I didn't see anything this trip and decided to pack up around noon and call it quits. We had a three-hour ride back home and I didn't want to hunt all day and be tired driving home. When we arrived back to the house and unpacked the truck Jerome and Jill arrived about an hour later from visiting with his folks. As soon as Jerome and Jill got situated, he made up an excuse to leave Jill behind so he could immediately hop on the train to visit his fiancée who lived in Atlanta. The next day Jill caught the bus heading back to Alabama. Later that evening, I took Melissa shopping and bought her new undergarments and uniforms for her new job that she'd be starting when she got back home. We lost track of time because her flight was leaving in three hours. When we arrived back to the house, she repacked her bags and I drove her to the airport. When Melissa landed, she began telling me how much fun she had and that she appreciated me for everything I did for her. Melissa started working the next day and Paul found a job working for the chicken plant. When Melissa got home after her first day on the job, she called me and let me know her work schedule. She told me that the brakes were worn down and was scraping the rotors. I knew that wasn't good so she went to the man who usually worked on her car and he told her that he could change the brakes for forty dollars. I knew she didn't have the money so I ordered the brakes online and sent her the money to pay the man for the work.

Melissa wasn't working for long and the holidays were approaching fast. I wasn't sure what she had planned for Christmas, but I felt that it was too soon to get together, besides I wanted her to begin saving money without spending a majority of it traveling. Melissa and I agreed to spend The New Years together instead. New Year's Eve I was in North Carolina awaiting her arrival but she called me and said that she had to wait because her job gave her a mandatory assignment. I understood so I wasn't upset and told her that we'll just wait until February and I'll fly out there for my birthday. Nevertheless, that evening Jerome asked me to work at the club with him as security detail for a few hours. I didn't mind because it gave me a few extra dollars in my pocket. When we get to the club, I noticed that Jerome had a firearm on his side, knowing that he's a convicted felon I was a little jarred because I realized that Jerome didn't give a damn about his freedom. I had my Pennsylvania concealed weapons permit which is honored by the state of North Carolina so my cousin who works as a bounty hunter stopped by and handed me a firearm to work with that night. When Jerome and I got back to the house we played spades, ate and I showered and called it a night.

The next morning, Melissa called me and her entire tone towards me changed as if I did or said something negative to her. I asked Melissa, "What's wrong? Why are you talking to me as if I did something to you?" Melissa responded, "You don't want me to go anywhere?" I was shocked because I always boosted her to do positive things and go places instead of always sitting in the house contemplating suicide or dealing with negative issues. In life we deal with all types of issues, situations, people and circumstances and therefore an outlet is always necessary. Melissa called me and became open about her current situation. She asked me if I knew a good lawyer that would be willing to go to court with her for a child support hearing. I suggested an attorney for her that she called and hired to represent her. I paid for the lawyer's travel expenses and accommodations. Melissa asked me to go to court with her and the lawyer, so I accompanied her for moral support. Melissa's husband never appeared in court so the Judge awarded her a temporary support order. Things worked out better than Melissa expected and I took Melissa, the lawyer, my mother, Jerome and Sharonda {Jerome's girlfriend} to dinner to help celebrate the victory. While we're eating Sharonda sparks up a conversation with Melissa and says, "You look familiar. Do you know a guy by the name Joe that lives in Georgia?" Melissa looks at me as if I didn't hear the question or paying attention. Melissa responded, "No, I don't know anyone in Georgia. I pretty much stay to myself." Sharonda adamantly responds, "I know I've seen you somewhere before." Melissa gave me a stare that pretty much let me know that she was uncomfortable with the questions. When I got in the car I explained to Melissa, "I don't care who you were involved with or met prior to me. We all have a past and that's perfectly okay just as long as you don't allow them to interfere with your present." When we left dinner, we stopped by the internet café to play a few games before we headed in for the evening.

The next morning, Melissa received a phone call from her father making sure she was okay. Melissa got dressed and I walked her to her car, kissed her and she left. Usually she'd call me to let me know that she made it safely to her destination, but not this time. When I called her phone, it went straight to voicemail, so I left a message. Melissa called me approximately five hours later when she was headed back to Georgia. I asked her, "Is everything okay with you? You're doing things out of the norm." Melissa responded, "There's so much on my plate that I'm dealing with that's driving me insane. I'll call you when I get home." "Not a problem", I answered.

There was so much going through my mind at this very moment. I began thinking about my last relationship I was in that the young lady was a bipolar schizophrenic and had multiple personalities. I wasn't going to ignore any red flags or signs this time around. Melissa kept her word and called me when she got home and situated. Melissa video called me when she was laying in the bed and both of her sons was in the room with her. Melissa was wearing a thong, a shear shirt with no bra. I asked Melissa to go in the bathroom but she acted as if she didn't understand the reason behind the question. Her oldest son, Paul was twenty-seven and looked at his mother and said, "Mom, Lamont's trying to get your attention to let you know that you need to put some clothes on in front of us." It was a very disturbing moment to be dressed like that in front of her adopted thirteen-year-old that experienced being sexually abused and a homosexual biological son. Melissa showed extreme signs of hate and jealousy towards her adopted daughter. On one of the road trips Melissa fed everyone but refused to feed the daughter. I told Melissa to stop mistreating her or allow her to live with her grandmother. Melissa refused to let either child go because that would mean that the kid's social security from the death of their biological mother would be given to someone else. Melissa only cared for the money she received, but did very little for those children. When I told her that she was mistreating those children, she immediately tried to justify her actions. Melissa's adopted thirteen-year-old son would always sleep in the same room with her and Melissa would fall video call me in the dark and the bed would be moving while Melissa would be making odd noises. Melissa would lay the phone down when she thought I fell asleep and would sleep with her adopted child. Melissa would always tell me how she'd catch her thirteen-year-old masturbating and that he's a spitting image of his father. Melissa was extremely upset and distraught that those children's father left her for someone else that she was on anxiety pills. The sad part about those children is that they were constantly being abused and nobody really cared. The little girl was labeled a schizophrenic and the boy was labeled mentally challenged and both of them were on medication.

When I visited Melissa for my birthday, I wanted to see the well-being of the children. Melissa lived in a two-bedroom apartment in the projects. Paul picked me up from the airport and we stopped by Doc's club in College Park, Ga. but he wasn't there. We waited about an hour because we wanted to time it perfect to get to Melissa's job to pick her up when she got off. When we got to the nursing home Paul texted her to let her know that we were there. Melissa ran out the building smiling and gave me a hug and a kiss. Melissa was wearing khaki pants and a burgundy collared shirt as her uniform. In my mind I was thinking, "Melissa has been lying to me from the beginning." Melissa clocked out and we were on our way to the apartment but stopped at Taco Bell to get a bite to eat. When we pulled up in the parking lot a few people were listening to music dancing, smoking marijuana and playing cards. We proceeded to walk upstairs to her apartment and when I walked through the door, I saw the young girl sleeping on the carpet without a blanket or sleeping bag. The living room was illuminated by the oven light in the kitchen. The thirteen-year-old boy was on the top bunk in the bedroom on the right side and the bedroom on the left belonged to Melissa. Once Melissa got in, she showered and got situated and then I took a shower and got ready for bed. In each bedroom there were a set of twin bunk beds and the only television in the place was in Melissa's room. Once we ate, we watched a little television before we went to sleep.

The next morning, Melissa had to work and the children had to go to school so Paul drove her to work and then dropped the children off to school. Paul had a few errands to run afterwards and he told me that he'd be back around noon to get me. I made sure that I was situated and dressed prior to noon because I had no idea what his plans were. I know it was my birthday week and I didn't expect anything outrageous or extraordinary, it was just an honor to spend it with people that I loved and cared about. Paul has always been polite and respectful towards me and he kept his adopted siblings in line. I realized that Paul spent more time with the children than

Melissa because he seemed to be the caretaker that took more time out with them because Melissa had other agendas. Melissa called me during her lunch break to see how I was doing and to let me know that she missed me. I let her know that I was doing well and that Paul and I were about to head out to grab a bite to eat. Paul and I headed out to a chicken spot and grabbed a sweet tea to drink and a small bucket of lemon peppered wings. When we left the chicken spot he stopped by a bakery and bought me a birthday cake. During the ride home Paul said, "I just wanted to say thank you for helping us out as a family and I hope my mother don't fuck things up with you." I replied, "I've searched for your mother for a number of years and I'm glad to have her back in my life. I also appreciate you for being by your mother's side and helping her out tremendously. What did you mean you hope she don't mess things up?" Paul said, "My mother loves attention and will do anything to get it. Anyone that she feels is getting more attention than her is a problem for her, that's why she dresses in revealing and tight clothing. I can see that you're a man of integrity and respect, that's why my grandmother likes you because she feels that you have entered my mother's life to guide her to the right path." "To be honest, I can only live my life as I know and enhance the positive qualities that your mother already possesses, anything else will be conflicting", I answered. When we arrived back to the apartment, I went into the bedroom to relax and Melissa video called me and asked me, "Hey baby. Can you call my supervisor and tell her that you're on leave for a few days to propose to me, so that I can have a minor vacation while you're here?" I replied, "Why do I need to lie to your supervisor? Just ask for those days off." Melissa gave me a calculated answer that really didn't make sense but I did things her way. I called Melissa's supervisor and told her exactly what Melissa asked of me. Melissa received the requested time off but in order to make things official she had to go back to work wearing an engagement ring. I knew that I wasn't going to buy a ring until I knew that she was who I desired to marry. Later that evening I rode with Paul to pick Melissa up from work. The moment Melissa got into the car she began ranting about how a few of her co-workers hated on her because of the shape of her body. Paul glanced at me as to say, "I told you." It didn't stop there because she started talking about how all the women were falling over the new male nurse. Paul looked at me again and began smiling as to say, "Your intention is to beat them out and receive his attention by any means necessary." I began telling Melissa, "You have to overlook things at times because you're not obligated to make friends at any job, just do your job." Melissa responded, "You're right."

When we got to the apartment Paul wanted to see the children's homework, made sure they ate and made them shower and brush their teeth prior to going to bed. Melissa was so worried about her co-workers gaining more attention than her that she called her sister to get some advice. Her sister told her exactly what I did. Melissa lie down in the bed and put her head upon my chest as we cuddled and began talking. I knew something was bothering her, but I didn't know what it was so I asked her, "Is everything okay with you?" Melissa answered, "I'm just tired of going through this nonsense with the children's father and these women on the job. It seems as if everyone and everything is coming against me." "Well, I'm not going against you and I've been there for you since we started communicating again and it seems like you're unappreciative at times", I replied. "Yes, you've truly been there for us and I apologize if it seems that I don't appreciate the things you've done", Melissa responded.

I woke up the next morning, to a few birthday cards and a box from Melissa by the bed. Melissa was in the kitchen putting candles on the birthday cake. I asked Melissa not to light the candles until I got showered and dressed so I'd be presentable. When I got dressed Melissa, Paul and the children entered the room singing happy birthday to me. I blew out the candles and immediately opened the cards from the children. The children stated, "How glad they were to have me in their lives and hope that I'd never leave them." The card brought tears to my eyes as I hugged them and told them that I'd always be there for them and only a phone call away. I opened the box that Melissa had for me and there were two beautiful shirts with tigers on the front. Melissa also treated me to a seafood restaurant for lunch where she got a little upset with the waitress for subconsciously saying, "Thank you baby" after she dropped her pen and I politely handed it to her. When we got inside of the car Melissa got upset at me all over again for handing the lady her pen that dropped. I told Melissa, "Thank you for a beautiful lunch, but I wasn't paying that lady any attention." While we were out, we stopped by Walmart to get a few items and she saw the engagement ring case and bought herself a thirty-nine-dollar cubic zirconia ring so that she'd be able to show her supervisor that she got engaged. When we got back to her apartment, she immediately called all of the children into the room so that she could stage me proposing to her. Paul recorded the entire mock proposal on his phone and then said, "I really hope that one day this becomes official." In an instant Melissa got upset because it wasn't real, but I had to remind her that she set the entire stage to convince her supervisor. I asked everyone to leave the room so that I could speak to Melissa and I didn't want the children to hear any negativity. I had to explain to Melissa that I never asked her for anything and all I've tried to do was deposit positive things inside of her to help make her life a little easier. I also told her that I see that she loves all types of attention and that's not good. Melissa began crying and saying, "I've been married four times and all of them were abusive. You're the only person that I ever desired to be with but you left me twenty-six years ago. How am I going to trust that you're here to remain? My heart wouldn't be able to take that. I'm already taking anxiety and medication for depression." "Melissa, I didn't search for you all of these years to enter your life and leave you high and dry. Since we've been together, I've noticed a few things that disturb me", I replied. "Things that disturb you like what?" Melissa responded. "Well, it disturbs me how you walk naked around these children that have been sexually abused and then go to bed wearing thongs and see through shirts. It also bothers me that you clearly wear clothes too small for you to wear that the moment you sit down your entire ass is out. It also disturbs me how you clearly mistreat your daughter but your teenage son receives an open-door policy. It bothers me that you feel the need to lie to me about your occupation, you're not nor have you ever been a registered nurse. I took it upon myself to research the entire national nursing database under all of your names and came up with nothing. I gave you months to come to me with the truth but you felt the need to continue feeding me the lies." Melissa looked at me with disgust and said, "You researched me?" "Yes, because things that you were telling me didn't add up. The uniform you needed wasn't that of a registered nurse but was that of a nurse assistant." Melissa looked at me and began cussing me out. The best thing was for me to pack my things and leave. Melissa looked at me and asked, "Can we have sex for the last time since you're leaving?" I looked at Melissa and said, "If pussy is all you have to offer me then you have nothing to offer me at all." I asked Paul if he could take me to the airport. Paul looked at me and saw the look of disgust on my face. Paul went into his mother's room and said, "Mom what did you do? Lamont has been nothing but nice to all of us since he's been in our lives. He helped us without questioning anything, he fixed your car or sent money when he wasn't able to be here, he provided when he didn't have to and on top of all of that he drove your attorney seven hours to help you cut the cost of your legal representation." I was shocked that he broke that down to her but she realized that I wasn't the bad guy. Melissa came to me crying asking me not to leave and that she's sorry for the things she said to me. I accepted her apology and took everyone to CiCi's Pizza for dinner. I had two days left before I had to catch a flight back home so I wanted to make the best of it, besides Melissa had to be back to work the next morning. When we got back to her apartment we showered and watched a movie, cuddled, had passionate sex and fell asleep.

    The next morning, Melissa kissed me before she left and the children didn't have to go to school. When I woke up and got situated, I asked the children "Are you hungry?" They answered, "Yes Sir. We had a ketchup sandwich." "You had what! A ketchup sandwich!" "Yes. Mom doesn't want us to open the box of cereal." I looked in the cabinet and said, "Get that box of cereal and eat it. I'll let your mother know that I told you to eat it." The teenage son smiled as if an Angel was there to fight for them or come to their aide. The daughter didn't hesitate to eat it because I know she was hungry and I was a form of relief from them being mistreated. Anyone could tell that these children were being mistreated but they accepted it and refused to say anything. When children have been consistently shifted from negative environment to negative environment, they conform to it and begin weighing their options. It's sad, horrific and unacceptable that any child has to accept physical, emotional and psychological abuse. I found out that there have been a few complaints to CPS {Child Protective Services} concerning Melissa but they've returned unfounded. Melissa was at work and called me more times than she ever did. She was used to telling me that she couldn't have her phone on her while at work or if they're caught on the phone they'll get in trouble. When Melissa got home, I was in the room watching television. Paul was making dinner and the children were refreshing their school work. When Melissa got situated, I asked her, "Why didn't you allow the children to open the box of cereal? Instead they resorted to eating ketchup sandwiches." Melissa responded, "They don't know how to eat a little of anything and I didn't want them to eat the whole box." I left it alone because I didn't want to get involved in a heated debate.

The next day, Melissa was off work and the children were home so we spent the day watching television. It was a few hours left before I had to head to the airport so Melissa and I used that time to have a heart to heart. Melissa stayed home with the children when Paul drove me to the airport and I called her when I got through the check point and got to my gate. Melissa thanked me again for being there for her and her family and I let her know that I really appreciated the time we shared and also thanked her for opening up to me because I wasn't going to judge her.

When I landed, I called Doc and Melissa to let them know that I made it home safely. After I got situated, I called Melissa and out of the blue she began attacking me about my last relationship. I told Melissa, "If that's what you received from what you've read from my book then your level of comprehension is fucked up." I began picking Melissa's brain and asked her, "Have Jerome reached out to you?"

Melissa responded, "Why would you ask me that?" That was a dead giveaway. I began replaying certain things back in my mind from the times Melissa came to the house in North Carolina, the time we went hunting and the time Melissa made a statement concerning Jerome telling a lie in the article about him being a close friend to Kobe Bryant's family. Melissa's cousin Frank and Jerome drove from North Carolina to Los Angeles promoting a casket that Frank designed for Kobe Bryant. Jerome only went in the event the casket was sold he'd get a piece of the proceeds. Anyway, Melissa tried her best to deflect from my question saying, "Why would I talk to your lying ass brother?" Immediately, I went to Facebook and pulled up her profile and to my surprise Jerome was pictured in her friends list. I took a screen shot and sent it to her and told her to never contact me again.

There comes a point in life when we have to accept people for who they are instead of constantly making excuses for them. I understand the religious concept of forgiveness, but when your life is at risk you can't afford to take any chances.

"Learn to accept people for who they are and stop trying to accept them for the potential that you see within them. Some people will never achieve the potential or credit you're giving them because of the lack of internal wisdom, low self-esteem, living in past hurts, trying their best to degrade you or trying to please others." - Lamont Bershawn.

Relationship 010:
"If your significant other chooses to believe someone else's word over yours without proof, documentation or validation; leave them completely alone. You might figure out the individual feeding them the bullshit is one of your relatives or friends that's envious of you." - Lamont Bershawn.

When Jerome contacted me, I sent him the photo while he was on the phone and told him, "Thank you for showing me exactly who I was involved with. You've done the same thing when I was with Stephanie and I think it's best that I consider you completely dead. You're a dangerous individual that will cause someone to throw their entire life away because you have absolutely nothing going for yourself. You're dead to me!!"

Don't ever deceive YOURSELF!!

YOU have aspirations, goals, ambitions, the power to dream, think and envision.

The moment you STOP is the moment you give your life away.

Your purpose is to make your dreams/ visions a REALITY!!

BEWARE though because there are people that you've allowed in your circle that are listening to your ideas, you're making public. These people are impostors whom you THOUGHT were your friends or close family members.

1) Why are they stealing your ideas?

2) Why have they decided to get closer to your "friends" and make them their very own?

3) Why are they trying their best to dismember or degrade you behind your back?

ANSWER:

Insecure "mutha fukkas" thrive on living in the confines of the lies they create for themselves and accept the lie as their reality. "NOTHING FROM NOTHING LEAVES NOTHING!"

The people that makes the decision to be-LIE-ve them and connect with them are better off with them, TRUST ME!

Iron sharpens iron as flies go hard for a pile of shit.

REMAIN FOCUSED or time will pass you by and you'll begin reflecting on your past only to realize that you've birthed so many millionaires or billionaires; but you're still at the beginning of the circle.

You've been wondering why you've been seeing the same old things, attracting the same type of folk and engaging in the same old conversations without evolving in your travels.

You've been on a solar powered Ferris wheel and didn't know it.

This is YOUR time, YOUR NOW.... MAKE YOUR LIFE WORK for YOU!

When situations occur that relieve you of some folk, ACCEPT IT!!

Don't ask questions, don't get upset, don't argue and don't worry but be EXTREMELY HAPPY. The vindictive will easily connect with its kind as with the schizophrenic, the liar or deceiver. The reason it's NOT as easy to connect with you is because your innermost radar can pick up on their bullshit! – Lamont Bershawn.

I now understand why people have said, "Jerome desires to be you so bad that he hates himself for his personal decisions. Be watchful and careful of his sadistic personality because he's eager to blame you for something in order to tarnish your character and reputation."

What I've come to realize is that in a blink of an eye a lie can turn your entire life upside down. This is why it's very easy for me to create my own family and disconnect from those individuals that aren't beneficial for me.

Please also be mindful of the word's family, relatives, brotherhood or sisterhood. Whether it's in a sorority, a fraternity, a religious organization or blood related; they'll all take advantage of you or literally screw you over. What am I saying, "TRUST NO ONE!"

"The enemy can't gain access into your life unless your "inner me" gives it access. Once you realize the enemy has gained access, then your "inner me" MUST begin to reject it in order to eject it." - Lamont Bershawn.

"BETRAYAL is the worst fucking sin; especially by those you once considered kin." - Alexander Hardy.

Mama's Boy

You think Eye'm soft because Eye stick close to my mother,
Failing to realize that she loves me like no other,
Don't fault me because your mother is no longer here,
If she were would you even care?

You live according to societies rules,
Neglecting the fact of the woman who gave you the necessary tools.
A mama's boy is not so bad at all,
So, grab your balls and continue standing tall.

When mama need, you're always there,
Just like she is for you so she'd have no fear,
You only get one mother so never forget,

Mama's Boy

Those calling you mama's boy relationship with their mother didn't mean shit.
Be watchful of those that criticize you through and through
Never turn your back on your mother she's the one that gave birth to you,
Life wouldn't exist if it wasn't for my mother,
Yet feeling some sort of way being called mama's boy by another!!

Take it as a badge of honor and one to be respected,
Did you notice the ones calling you mama's boy are the ones most rejected?
They're sitting back wondering if you'll ever leave mama's side,
Not understanding she's the true "ride or die."

Eye know time is winding up and mama will be no more,
When that time comes it will hurt me to my core.
Just knowing the time shared with mama Eye did my best,
Embracing every moment until it's time for her eternal rest.

Until then watch and see,
When you look up it will be my mama and me.
Just seeing mama being able to smile,
Makes my heart want to run a mile.

She battled cancer, a tumor and always fought for me,
Fuck societies rule my mother she'll always be.
Mama, Eye know you're tired but you refused to see us lack,
Enjoy living your life because Eye got your back.
- Lamont Bershawn {original piece}

    Why is it that according to society rules at a certain age man can't express unconditional and undying love for their mother in the midst of their significant other? If in a relationship, why does it cause tension or problems between your significant other and your mother? Is there such a thing as having a "favorite" child when multiple children are involved by the same parents? Of course, there's a favorite although many parents will answer, "I love all of my children just the same."

In order for a seed to grow it must be watered and receive the necessary nutrients.

The amazing thing about us as individuals, we all start as a seed but most of us have never been cultivated or validated.

We go throughout life with our parents/ guardian train of thought or whatever life experiences have allowed us to absorb.

We conform to society rules and regulations on how our life is supposed to be without taking note that we all have different perspectives, views and experiences.

Right now, someone is feeling worthless or on the brink of committing suicide. I want you to know that you're important and that your life is very meaningful.

You have adapted enough, helped enough, prayed long enough and have lived in misery long enough.

The VOICE is clearly speaking to your heart, your mind and your gut, "It's time to take your life/ power back!!" (You've lent it out long enough for the benefit of others)!! - Lamont Bershawn.

    I remember being a toddler wanting to always be creative in everything I set out to do. I wanted to learn how to build and fix things like my father and on the other hand I wanted to learn how to cook and bake like my mother. I had two brothers and in the beginning we were close, but eventually we had to follow our own ambitions. My mother made sure that she kept a family atmosphere which meant that we'd eat dinner together sitting at the table or we'd have an educational hour of learning and an hour of playtime. My father worked for the Energy Company which took up the time he allowed. At the time I had no idea about the financial classification of a family nor did I know the annual salary of any occupation. All I knew is what seemed popular which were police officers, fire fighters, doctors and nurses. My father didn't want us to go to any babysitter and he wanted my mother to consistently watch us. There were a few people that my mother trusted us with besides my grandparents. I really couldn't wait until my brother Kurt became of age so that he could watch us. Jerome and I listened to him; besides he'd eat all types of gummy or chewy candy. He seemed to always have a brown paper bag full of goodies.

Growing from boys into men, we'd always respect our parents not only because it was required but also because we were cultivated into doing so. We had our differences and we were constantly challenged to think prior to making a decision or choice.

Kurt loved music so much that he was consistently in church trying to build the next "Winans" musical gospel group or a soloist that could grab the hearts of the people. Being a senior in high school Kurt adopted a little freshman as his little brother and he brought him home with him. Kurt's little brother from high school name was Wayne. When we met Wayne, he was a little shy but had an amazing spirit and voice. Wayne was a few months younger than me and Jerome so he'd hang around us more than he did Kurt. Wayne would sit around and listen to Luther Vandross, Michael Jackson, Stevie Wonder and Donny Hathaway just to name a few of the greats and Wayne would harmonize with the song and make it his very own. Wayne was determined to be a great singer that would be recognized by the world. Wayne's grandmother would call every day to see how Wayne was doing. Wayne's father lived in New Jersey which was far from his school and his mother was strung out on drugs and his grandmother was up in age and wanted Wayne to be in the midst of a family that would treat him like their very own. When my mother bought things for us Wayne was definitely included. When we went to visit our grandmother's home, Wayne was also included. While Wayne was in school, he wouldn't go to recess like most of the children. Instead Wayne met up with three other singers in order to form a singing group. Needless to say, a few years later Wayne and his group became recognized by Motown Records and are one of the hottest male groups around today.

Jerome on the other hand was still trying to define himself through martial arts like his Sifu or impersonating a law enforcement agent. Anything Jerome felt necessary to do just to mimic his Sifu, he did.

Forgiveness is a part of the keys to opening the door to a successful life:

As Eye've gotten older, Eye "real-eyes" that there are levels to forgiving or forgiveness. It's hard for some people to say, "I'm sorry or I apologize" but they'll reveal their forgiveness through their actions.

We must take note that everyone has a different set of rules according to their raising/ upbringing. Sometimes it's easier to accept what we can get from a person instead of expecting them to apologize "our" way.

When we sit back and analyze the situation, we've disregarded, cut off or disconnected from someone that looked up to us. They were learning how to become a better individual just trying to mimic YOU!! - Lamont Bershawn.

In all of my year of living I've never felt the need or desire to turn my back on my mother or any woman that I've grown to love for that matter. I understand that the Bible says that a man and woman shall leave their parents and cleave unto each other, but that comes after the marriage.

Over 400 years we watched our women become door mats to our oppressor, degraded at all cost and become their releasing tool and we did nothing. It hurts my heart to hear young black men degrading our women in music for a paycheck.

Allow me to let you know about the woman I call mother.

She is the first God{dess} that I was introduced to. It was her option to introduce me to another God through religious doctrine or scripture.

You're MY mother:

A Powerful source to creation. A lady that nurtures, cares, loves, respects and protects her own. A woman that builds her house from the remaining fabric of a cloth that becomes a fortress or refuge for her young, that nothing will be able to penetrate. Your guidance, your strength, your intuition, your chastisement of love, your wisdom will forever be instilled in your children as a compass of direction and protection.

You stand in GREATNESS!! Watching your youth grow before your very eyes as you continue to honor them as they learn by the instructions you've given them, as they evolve with the change of the new day, as they project the undying love through their daily living as the seasons change, as they honor you for giving them life.

You are honored as the Queen Mother, you are respected as Empress Educator, you are raised and praised as Mother of Creation. Every day we bow with humility to honor your walk. The times you covered us when your immune system was low; the times you were wounded, yet you exemplified strength; the times you felt like giving up, yet the look at your children gave you the tenacity to continue on; the times you were in battle with so many things that were unaware to us, yet you knew you had to be the warrior of hope.

It's because of you MOTHER, that we have life and have it more abundantly. It's because all of the "HELL" you caught that provided us with a life of "Heaven." It's because you made the choice to carry us through the entire term and refused to kill the dream that would one day become a great Philosopher, Actor, Scientist, Doctor, Police officer, fire fighter, Author, Teacher, Astronaut, President or friend.

We see you drawing weary and need a day of rest; We know you're tired because you've given your very best. Your Excellency, you have tirelessly fought for us through every fiber of resounding power; the least I could do is give you a single flower. No words of gratitude will ever be enough, a bouquet of flowers seems so traditional, a box of chocolates just won't do. I honor your life today and always because it was you that carried me through!! – Lamont Bershawn.

My Mother Never Failed Me Poem

The strength of my mother you could never see,
Why? Because you weren't privileged to be born as me.
Whether my spoon was copper, platinum, silver or brass,
My mother raised us with dignity, integrity and class.

My mother taught me how to cook, bake, iron, clean and sew,
I'd never have to depend on a woman for anything; You know!
Mom would take a piece of fabric or cloth and make me an outfit,
Folk would be asking, "How did she accomplish that shit?"

Lamont Bershawn

My mother covered and protected her children and we never begged for bread,
Between my mother and my grandmother, we always kept a level head. Through all of her trials, tribulations, setbacks and faults,
My mother groomed us into becoming respectable adults.

My mother didn't have to turn a trick like the now a day chic,
The only thing on their mind is getting the dick,
That Proverbs 31 woman, that Nubian Queen and Black Goddess,
Let's me know daily that I'm truly blessed.
I'm not the product of the projects but of a middle-class neighborhood,
What I've learned is that within us all is the power to do good.
Don't ever tell me that my mother failed me,
When we're a portion of the same tree called the black family.

Degradation is rooted in our blood and veins,
This is why it's easy for us to constantly change lanes.
We impregnate you and leave you high and dry,
Marry a white woman and think we've reached the sky.

Please black sister, give me a fucking break,
I'm a true king and have taken all I'm going to take,
Being wounded by every hand I'm not your enemy,
It will never resonate in my heart that my mother nor you ever willfully failed me!
- Lamont Bershawn. {Original Piece}!!

"I'm Still Your Brother"

Ever since birth it was a joy to see,
Another person in the world looking exactly like me,
God didn't bless mom with one at a time but two,
Somehow, he knew we'd need each other to make it through.

We're supposed to be here for each other,
Why? Because you were introduced to me as my brother,
Together we definitely could be a force of one,
But the things you've done to me makes me turn my back and run.

Lamont Bershawn

Where did things go wrong in my perspective?
When you allowed pussy and looks to be your only objective.
Even when your girlfriends blatantly told you that I was the better-looking twin,
You tried to kill me because you wanted my life to end.

Twenty-five years later you're doing the same old shit,
In the back of my mind I'm wondering when you'll ever quit.
When will it ever hit you that I'm your brother,
And you ought to stop living life like I'm your competitor.

Telling lies on me still won't set you free,
When your entire catalog is made up of fake degrees.
The friends you claim know where you lack,
That's why in your face they'll smile but laugh at you behind your back.

Hurt me to my heart that you'd make a deal,
Signed your soul away at your own free will.
Making a statement keeping our eldest brother incarcerated,
What the hell were you thinking or were you just frustrated?

He's now fighting the fight of his life,
Leaving behind two children and a wife.
I still don't get why you are so God damned mad,
It's not like you lived a life that was so bad.

We grew up doing things that others only dreamed of,
Our parents made a sacrifice out of love.
Why is it embedded in the back of your head?
That you wished your twin brother was dead.

I decided to write this book to reveal total truth,
Up to this moment stemming from our youth.

"I'm Still Your Brother"

Thanks be to God that I'm your brother,
And I don't look at you as my competitor.

Go ahead and live your life full of fabrications,
People will begin reading about your convictions.
When the smoke clears and the fake friends leave you for another,
That's when you'll realize that I'm still your brother.

- Lamont Bershawn.

"ACKNOWLEDGEMENTS"

To my loving mother, Dorothy Burno. You're the first Goddess that Eye recognized. You carried me a full life term without ever giving up on me. It was through your pain that Eye saw the real strength to never give up on my dreams or visions. You taught me that life was valuable and Eye only had one to live, so make my stamp on the world.

Thank you for loving me and giving me LIFE!!
Eye'll always love you mom!!
I dedicate my everything to YOU!!

To my brother, Dr. Dennis Spencer. You've inspired me to follow my dream and never give up. Thank you for taking the time to lead and guide me as a big brother. Your priceless investment of wisdom alone has made me a better individual. You know without a doubt that you'll forever be able to count on me. This book made it possible for everything within me to finally speak the words, "I'm FREE!"

To my extended family, The Barg- Walkow Family. You've been there for my mother well over twenty years. You've engraved a very special place in my heart that's irreplaceable. Thanks so much for your never-ending support.

To my deceased "Brother from another mother", Alexander Hardy. Words could never explain my heartfelt gratitude and appreciation.

You tend to bring the joy and laughter out of me even in the midst of my heartache and pain. The countless number of hours that were spent on the phone was always uplifting. You painted a clear picture of my path when it all seemed so blurry. We have so much in common that you even began accepting my mother as your very own. Eye appreciate you from the bottom of my heart brother.

To my photographer, Shalilyah Henry. Thank you for everything! You've brought life to places that I thought were dead and renewed my spirit!!

To my social media family, thank you for allowing me inside your hearts and minds. Thank you for your loving support!

To my legal team, thank you for fighting for me and bearing with me.

"I'm Still Your Brother"

People rarely see me smile because I'm always focused. When so many things in your life is coming together like pieces to a puzzle. There are many folks that placed bets on your life and expect you to fail or fall apart.

FAILURE ISN'T AN OPTION!!

When I sit back and look back over the things that I've conquered that should have sent me to an Insane Asylum. The things that could have sent me to my grave and the people that turned their backs on me all I can do is smile.

I can honestly say, "I appreciate everyone that became the wind beneath my wings that held me up in my weakest moments!" -Lamont Bershawn.

"I'm Here for You Brother"

What is it that you're trying to do to me?
Do you really think that I'm that filthy?
Born in this world with melanin in my skin,
And you expect me to hate the skin that I'm in?

"I'm Here for You Brother"

Babies are born as innocent creatures,
Not one thought concerning their features,
I have it hard enough being a black man,
Why is it your desire to take things out of my hand?

Constantly praying to a God that just didn't care,
The bible said he had skin of bronze and wooly hair,
Figured out it was the God of the oppressor,
Now I know why you're the aggressor.

You were taught that you were better than me,
Hell, your dad works for a fortune 500 company.
Things stacked against me on each and every side,
It was expected of me to go run and hide.

I want you to know that I recognized this shit,
It was instilled within me to never give up or quit,
My backbone can stand all forms of pressure,
Doesn't matter the weather or temperature.

My dear brother I can feel your pain,
Even when the sun is shining, you're experiencing the rain.
24 hours in a day from dusk 'til dawn,
I'll always be here for you my brother my name is Lamont Bershawn.

www.ingramcontent.com/pod-product-compliance
Lightning Source LLC
Chambersburg PA
CBHW020533080526
44583CB00013B/850